Disruptive Leaders

PROFITING FROM SIGNS FROM THE FUTURE

JOHN SUTHERLAND

John Sutherland is a strategic innovation practitioner, sought after speaker, innovation tools maker and founder of Ennova Inc. He works with executives across a wide variety of industries transforming how they think and behave to capture the opportunities available in the exponential age we call the 21st century. The discoverer of the universal language of value creation John has translated this and other value creation discoveries into The Shared Clarity System™. Through the power of common language and visualization this structured conversation tool-set empowers leadership teams to:

1. See more clearly, and interpret with greater insight, the technological and behavioral changes outside their industry norm.
2. Translate those insights into compelling new user scenarios.
3. Determine faster and with greater precision, how to best shape their business to exploit those scenarios.
4. Implement faster the resultant change with less risk and greater rewards.

He previously published On Signals: Profiting from signs from the future. This companion book summarizes the key thoughts outlined in Disruptive Leaders. It was the world's first business book published in tweet form and a PDF version is available for download at www.johnsutherlandbooks.com

ISBN: 0989293629
ISBN-13: 9780989293624

Contents

Acknowledgments

This book sprang out of the urging of many colleagues and peers. My special thanks to Alexander Manu for sharing his wisdom and knowledge with me. Many of the value-based tools described here are based upon his ideas in *Disruptive Business*. I'm grateful for the opportunity to have worked with you and look forward to our future collaborations.

I want to thank the seventeen business leaders I interviewed prior to the start of this book. You helped me understand my audience and are listed in the appendix. Thanks to the 129 people from twenty-six countries who made comments on my book's website. They too are listed in the appendix.

Thank you to Breanne Hingley, my graphic designer, who created all the images in this book. It is much easier to explain complex concepts when a simple image is available. Thanks to John Harten, my editor who gave me insights into idea-flow when I needed it.

I'd also like to thank Alexander Osterwalder. You showed me how to see life through a canvas and a common language.

To Katie Richardson, with whom I have worked these last three years; thanks for your insights and constant reminders to make it simple. You helped me push this project forward.

Finally, a hat tip to George Mohacsi, President and CEO of Foresters Inc. In 1995, as I described how Cirque du Soleil was an innovative form of entertainment, George made the following comment: "That's all well and good, John, but we are an insurance company and I can't see how a new kind of circus applies to us." That comment started me on the journey of how to interpret signals that fall outside the norm. Thanks for stumping me.

Dedication

To my wife Ginette, with whom I have been blessed to have lived with these last thirty-seven years. She makes my accomplishments possible. To my two sons Marc and Justin, in whom I take great pride in who they are as men and what they have achieved.

To my grandchildren, Tristan, Owen, and Graham. After all, it is their future we are talking about.

Prologue: What Are Signals?

It's 1492. They call you Manobo the Water Runner because you used to run on the river rocks as a boy. You live on the shores of San Salvador and are preparing to take the canoe out to sea to catch today's fish. For all twenty-five years of your life you've lived here. Later this month you expect to be invited to join the elders in the ancestors' hut. There you will learn the sacred rituals of speaking with your ancestors and the secrets of the world. But that's all in your future. Right now, the morning sky is red in the east and you have to hurry to make your catch before the storms come.

But when you look up, you see a strange cloud on the horizon. You wonder why it's moving in a different direction than the others. Transfixed, you stare as it comes closer, not realizing that the world upon which you depend will soon be gone forever. You've always known, as thousands of generations before you have known, that the spirits talk through the ancestors, that they tell the elders when the rains will come and let them know which murders need to be revenged. You know all the tricks to making tools, as these have been passed down from generation to generation. You know these tools represent the finest implements man can make. You know there is a rhythm and flow to life, with rituals and sacred objects that bring meaning to everyone in the village, protecting them from the dangers of the world.

That's all about to change. A canoe far larger than anyone could ever have imagined will land on your shores that day. Men—or perhaps gods—will disembark. Your elders will no longer be the most important or powerful men in the village. Your axes will pale in comparison to their weapons. A new god will displace your ancestors. Everything you knew about how to succeed in life is about to be turned upside down.

You didn't ask for this change. You don't want this change. But you don't have a choice. It's coming and you can't stop it. You didn't realize it when you saw the strange cloud, but you were looking at your future.

Signals are just that, signs from our future. They represent the changes brought on by people, objects, and ideas that affect our lives. We've always known about signals. In the 800's in Northern Europe, peasants would run from villages when they saw smoke columns on the horizon. They knew it meant the Vikings were coming to rape, pillage, and kill. Likewise, villagers on the Pacific islands would run into the hills when the oceans receded, since it was a sure sign of an approaching tsunami.

Those were the big events that caused disruption. They were rare and catastrophic. We still watch for signals. Incoming enemies and hurricanes are tracked by satellite, earthquakes are detected by sensors.

> **Key thought: Signals are signs from the future about change to come.**

In transitioning from an agricultural society to a modern one, we've increased the complexity of our world a thousand times over. Two hundred years ago, the world lived in rural societies bounded by the limits of human, animal, water, and wind power. We communicated through speech and writing. For thousands of years, life was like that.

Change happened slowly, across decades, even centuries. Now we live in an urban world reliant upon industrial power, one in which we can communicate instantly around the globe. As the complexity of the world has increased, so too has the speed of change. Stock markets plummet 30 percent in seconds. The opposite is true too. Companies—think Twitter, Facebook, and Instagram—grow into billion-dollar organizations in just a few years. We live in a world of "from nothing to gigantic overnight."

Here's an example of the speed of change, which can be seen as an opportunity for some and a disruption to others. On April 29, 2003, Apple launched the iTunes store. Five short years later it had grown into the largest purveyor of music in the United States, displacing the music giants of the time. That disruption of music distribution is nothing compared to the onslaught about to arrive.

It's common knowledge that we are moving rapidly from the industrial to the information age. But did you know that along with this transition there are twelve other *exponential technologies* that will also bring their share of disruption and opportunity[1]? They are the mobile Internet, artificial intelligence, the Internet of things, cloud technology, advanced robotics, driverless vehicles, next-generation genomics, energy storage, 3-D printing, advanced materials, advanced oil and gas exploration and recovery, and renewable energy.

Here are five examples of these technologies:

1. **Machine Problem Solving**. Artificial intelligence is already figuring out solutions we can't conceive of for the problems we face. IBM has built a cancer diagnostic capability based on its Watson artificial intelligence. It has found solutions to cancer treatment that the best oncologists at Sloan Kettering did not know about.

2. **Additive Manufacturing**. Home-based 3-D printing already prints out jewelry, toys, and even gunstocks in stainless steel. You can download a 3-D CAD design online and watch a YouTube video on how to set it up. Researchers are building a prototype to print a home in less than a day. People in Britain have already received access to printed jawbones for use in facial transplants. Others are printing out kidney cells.

3. **Synthetic Life**. The team at the J. Craig Venter Institute has created the world's first synthetic life form, a cell programmed with artificial, computer-generated DNA[2]. The future holds the promise of man-made bacteria that churn out biofuels or consume cholesterol in our bodies. These are just two among a million other possibilities.

4. **Advanced Robotics**. Advances in robotics mean our grandchildren will probably never learn to drive, as transportation will be driverless. The Baxter Robot from Rethink Robotics is programmable by anyone though simple gestures and motions. The future holds the promise of robots that cook and clean.

5. **Intelligent Manufacturing**. Nanotechnology builds lighter, stronger, intelligent materials to solve medical, construction, and manufacturing problems from the inside out. Researchers at the University of Florida (UF) have developed a nanoparticle that has shown 100 percent effectiveness in eradicating the hepatitis C virus.[3]

Why Exponentially Growing Technologies Matter

Leaders born before 1980 grew up in a linear world in which innovation was measured by year-over-year improvement. For example, the first land speed record was established in 1898 at 65 mph by an electric automobile. It topped out in 1997 at 760 mph by a jet engine car. That twelve times increase in speed took ninety-nine years. By comparison, the world's first laptop, the 1983 Osborne computer, began with a processing speed of 4MhZ. By 2013, the MacBook Pro featured a 6GhZ processor. That 1500 times increase in speed only took thirty years. While cars improved about 1.25 percent every year, computer processors have doubled their processing capacity every two years. All of our business systems were designed and built in a linear age of 1 to 2 percent improvement. Yet we live in the exponential age where improvements double every two years or so.

Where Is All This Headed?

Today, based solely on the transition to the information age, we are already witnessing the disruption of media companies. Publishers, music companies, movie companies, and their up-stream suppliers and customers are all under assault. A similar disruption is starting in education (with the Khan Academy) and in medicine (with health-related apps and IBM's Watson), to name but a few key areas.[4]

After these and other exponential technologies arrive, everything will be open to disruption: medicine, manufacturing, education, transportation, professional services, farming, mining, energy, and government. Is any one of these areas safe from the disruptive capabilities of these exponential advances?

And what happens when we combine robotics with artificial intelligence? That's happening already in Google's development of the driverless car. What about when we combine artificial intelligence with 3-D printing, or the nanotechnology that monitors functions with today's digital smart phones?

Some of these possibilities are here now, some soon to arrive, and some over the horizon. No matter. The list goes on and on across all walks of life. Each one portends change, a disruption of the norm. Collectively, they lead to the same destination: disruption on a massive scale across all elements of our society. At the front line of this change are business owners whose offerings and business models will come under attack from more agile entities that embrace these signs from the future.

At the same time as disruption arrives, new industries will be created by those who engage with the capabilities these technologies bring. Ten years ago, none of the following multibillion dollar companies and products existed: Google, Facebook, Twitter, LinkedIn, Blackberry, and Apple's iPhone, iPad, and iTunes. Those are just the companies in the realm of computer technology and Internet business. More importantly, none of them were predicted.

Tragically, most of us are blind to these signals, trapped like Manobo in our own personal perspective. Like him, we have only three choices in dealing with such changes: ignore them, fight them, or embrace them.

Why Are So Many Leaders Blind To These Signals?

Everyone lives in the present. Leaders are responsible to change organizations so they sustain themselves and grow. As such, leaders are tasked with guiding their enterprises into the future. While leaders live in the present, they work on the future. How well they do their work on the future determines the enterprise's success.[5]

In over twenty-five years of consulting with 100s of businesses across dozens of industries, I've learned one inescapable truth: most business leaders work within the norms of the industry and rarely, if ever, think about disrupting it. They plan, encourage, demand, and reward their organizations based on the belief that the future is an extension of the past. Very few are skilled at reading signs from the future further out than the next planning period, which for most is between one and three years. They all hold tightly to a hidden, unspoken, never-discussed belief. Simply put, they believe their futures are going to be a projection of their past and present. Bigger, stronger, faster and better, of course, but a projection nonetheless.

Yet that belief flies in the face of thousands of years of evidence and millions of examples. Were the iPhone, Facebook, FedEx, calculus, writing, and the printing press a better, stronger projection of the past?

Of course not. The leaders behind these inventions, discoveries, methods, and businesses didn't extend what others were doing. Their inventions acted as disruptors, changing the norms of how people accomplished their tasks and duties by providing new ways of doing them. In creating these inventions that acted as disruptors of human behavior, they *created* a new future. In doing so, they became disruptive leaders.

It's worth repeating. The people behind all the above didn't react to a future flowing toward them. They created a new future for themselves and those that followed.

The business conclusion is inescapable. The most important strategic choice we make as leaders is whether to *react* to the future as it arrives or whether to *make* it. Are you a *future taker* or a *future maker*?

All other strategic choices we make are subservient to this choice.

This book is written for dreamers, inventors, entrepreneurs, and other assorted game-changers who want to make their futures. Tired of spending fruitless energy on incremental improvements soon matched by competitors, they seek to leapfrog their competitors. They wish to lead their organizations to a place of sustainable differentiation and create strong barriers to entry behind them. No more do they want to expend effort on upholding the status quo. To be new leaders in the twenty-first century, they embrace the glorious, disruptive future that awaits us all.

What does the book cover?

To become a *future maker* you need to become a *disruptive* leader. Disruptive leaders are those who:

1. Understand how disruption occurs and follow the rules for successful disruption.
2. Read the signs of potential disruptors to find the ones relevant to their situation.
3. Evaluate the future based on its degree of uncertainty to find relevant barrier-to-entry opportunities.
4. Overcome their own personal internal antibodies created by success and expertise. (Internal antibodies are our fight or flight responses caused by things outside our norms).
5. Adopt disruptive story-telling as a core competency.
6. Add a disruptive mindset to how they view the world.

Chapter 1: The Universal Impact

OVERVIEW

We may think that new technologies or methods that disrupt our norms are all different. Surprisingly, they are not. They all follow a single, universal pattern in how they impact humankind.

> **Key Thought: All disruptions, good and bad, impact humankind in a universal way.**

As a disruptive leader, you need to embrace, engage with, and ultimately view the world through this universal disruption impact. Doing so will open your eyes to opportunities you were previously blind to and expose why your current offerings either do, or do not, create the kind of customer stickiness you desire.

If nothing else, it will make you a hit at parties when you describe how the advent of FedEx, the 1339 printing press, and insulin followed a common pattern in their impact on humankind.

Universal Disruption Impact

It's nine o'clock in the morning. You just woke up and suddenly realize that it's your best friend's birthday. She lives five miles away and you need to wish her happy birthday. If you live in a city in most parts of the world, no problem. You can call her on the phone, Skype her, tweet her, text message her, send a card, take the bus, go by car, ride a bicycle, or send flowers. If you live in some parts of rural Africa, your options are severely limited. You can walk or go by car. That's about it.

In both cases you have the same desire: to wish your best friend a happy birthday. What changed was the environment in which you found yourself. It's the environment that provides us the behavioral options we choose from to express our desires. This is what I call the *behavior space*, namely, the sum of all behaviors employed by users in the expression of their desires and goals. In large cities filled with technologies and objects, we have hundreds of options to express our desires. In rural areas, these options are limited and so too are our behaviors.

> **Key thought: The environment in which we live shapes our behaviors.**

It was always so. Looking back over history, we see a steady progress of inventions, each one adding to the list of behavior space options we could select from to express our desires. Here's a brief description of some of the inventions that helped us solve the problem of wishing our friend happy birthday.

With the domestication of horses for riding in Kazakhstan around 3500 BC, we could ride a horse to visit our friend. With the invention of mail services in Persia in 55 BC, we could send a letter instead. The invention of the telephone in 1876 allowed us to wish her happy birthday over the phone, with only our voice doing the traveling. These inventions allowed new behaviors to emerge: riding horses, writing letters, and phoning people. The inventions disrupted existing behavioral norms, allowing new behaviors to emerge, and over time, there developed new behavioral norms. *Behavioral norms* are simply the regular and habitual behaviors exhibited by individuals or groups in the expression of their desires.

Listed below are different communication inventions and their approximate date of invention. Each one gave us a new behavior we could use to solve the problem of communicating with someone outside of shouting distance.

Table 1: Communication disruptors and their approximate date of invention

Riding Horses	3500 BC	Letters by Mail	55 BC
Telegraph	1833	Bicycle	1839
Subway	1863	Phone	1876
Car	1881	E-mail	1971
Cell phone	1979	Skype	2003
Facebook	2004	YouTube	2005
Twitter	2006	Facetime	2010

Some of these inventions involved different ways to transport ourselves, some transported physical messages, and some transported our voices, images, or text. Each one of these added to our *behavior space*.

This pattern, through which a disruptor adds to our behavior space, holds true not only for our desire to communicate, but for all other desires as well. As human beings, we share common desires. Whether one is a member of the Yali Tribe in New Guinea or a soccer mom in Paris, we all want to:

- Love
- Be loved
- Get ahead
- Protect our families
- Be with our friends
- Be the best we can be

Maslow's hierarchy of needs[6] applies to everyone.

> **Key Thought: Human desires are common.**
> **The behaviors we manifest to express those desires are not.**

Remember this party question? "What albums would you take if you were marooned on a deserted island?" As a party question to get someone to prioritize the music and songs they like best, it's quite effective. However, as a practical question, it's meaningless. Deserted islands don't have electricity or power generators. Whatever device you brought with you would soon drain its batteries and you would be left with only the sounds of birds and the sea to accompany you.

We don't think about these utilities in the course of our day-to-day lives. They are mostly invisible to us. Pity the poor freshwater plant workers. No one ever thanks them for providing clean water to us 24-7. But we sure do complain when they don't.

We take clean water for granted, as we do most things in our modern lives: electricity, light bulbs, the Internet, mobile phone service, gas stations, cars, ball point pens, insulin, stoves, the equality of persons, mail service, voting, elevators, and all the other conveniences of life. More importantly than the fact that we take for granted the items, ideas, and processes of the modern world, we take for granted the personal behaviors these conveniences provide. Compare the list of the disruptors below and ask yourself the following question: "Which world would you rather live in, the *before* or *after*?"

Table 2: Behavior Manifestations from Modern Disruptors

Item	Behavior before	Behavior after
Water treatment plants	Get water from river or well	Turn on tap
Electricity, light bulbs	Burn candles, oil for light	Turn on switch
Internet	Find information from printed text	Surf the net
Mobile phone	Find pay phone	Call instantly
Cars	Saddle and look after horses	Turn on and go
Ball point pens	Use ink wells	Write anywhere
Insulin	Control diet, slow death	Inject insulin, productive life
Stoves	Cook over fires	Cooking controlled
Equality of persons	Discrimination, slavery	Freedom and equality
Mail service	Communicate face-to-face	Communicate over long distances
Voting	Subject to whims of ruler	Choose the ruling class
Elevators	Walk up stairs	Ride up

> ## Key Thought: Disruptors create new behaviors.

Each one of the above items, be it an object, an idea, a service, or a process, had the same impact. They enabled new behaviors to emerge. Until they arrived, certain behaviors were not available to us. Until the elevator was invented you *had* to walk up the stairs. There was no other choice. Its behavior did not exist because the object (the disruptor) did not exist.

> ## Key Thought: Disruptors can be objects, ideas, or processes.

In our daily lives, we rarely see the behavioral implications of all the objects and ideas in our life. We don't look at the cement sidewalk and contemplate the behavioral change paving the streets made, or how bricks changed the way we create buildings.

Each new addition not only added a new behavior, it also added new words. When a new disruptor arrives, we need to explain it. To explain it, we invent new words to describe the technology or the behavior it enables. For example, in 1839, when describing the invention of the bicycle, we didn't say, "I rode to see you on this machine that has two metal wheels on a frame that I push with my legs."[7] Instead, we invented a new term, *bicycle*, and we borrowed the verb "to ride" from the then-common experience of riding a horse. In the case of Alexander Graham Bell's invention, they called it a *telephone*. Its new behavior space was called *the phone call*. Imagine for a moment what it would be like to describe a phone call without using the word *phone*. Disruptors do that. They so change our behaviors that we invent words to describe the disruptors and the behaviors that they enable.[8]

> **Key Thought: Disruptors cause new words to be invented.**

The first sign that a signal might represent a potential disruptor is the volume of new words that surround it. It is our first glimpse into the power of the disruptor and the fact that it has happened outside our frame of reference. Each of the disruptors this book discusses has its own language. Additive manufacturing, machine problem solving, advanced robotics, intelligent manufacturing, and synthetic life all have their own language and terms to describe their impact. Yet they all follow the universal disruptive impact.

We believe we have free will. We believe we can behave the way we wish. And that's true, except when we find ourselves on a deserted island. Then we can't behave in the way we wish. We are limited to choosing behaviors from the behavior universe determined by the environment in which we find ourselves.

> **Key thought: The environment in which we find ourselves determines our behavior universe.**

A *behavior universe* is the totality of behaviors available to express human desires in any given environment and time. The history of humankind has been an endless cycle of disruptors, each one adding their behavior space to the behavior universe. Over time, these new behaviors create a new behavioral norm. Finally, they become so accepted that they become invisible. The delight we first experienced at the disruptor's introduction becomes so commonplace that it becomes invisible. Are you delighted at the idea of making a phone call? Or is it simply normal?

Figure 1: The Universal Value Creation Cycle

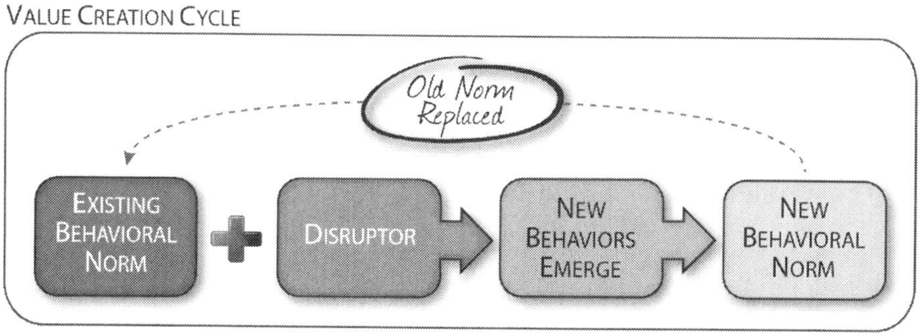

VALUE CREATION CYCLE

Conclusions for the Disruptive Leader

1. Disruptors change how we behave, how we do things. They enable new behaviors to emerge.
2. If your offering is not new, or has never changed the behavioral norm sometime in the past, then it is, or will become, a commodity.
3. As a disruptive leader, recalibrate your perspective to see the world, first and foremost, through the lens of behavior change.
4. Ask constantly, "How will my ideas allow new behaviors to emerge and enable new ways to express human desires?"

Exercise: Identifying Disruptors

1. Go outside, stand on the grass, and look at everything around you. Anything that is not natural was once a disruptor created by man.
2. Take an item, like an asphalt road, and imagine what life was like before it existed. Think of all the new behaviors that came from that invention.

3. Do the same for the telephone pole or the ball point pen someone is using.
4. Form the habit of looking at objects and processes from a behavior-change perspective, thinking about the behaviors that existed before and those that exist after.

Chapter 2: Disruptors and Signals

OVERVIEW

Where do ideas for disruption come from? They arrive from the signals of new technologies and behaviors that reside outside our organization's normal field of reference.

We are bombarded with signals every day. Some matter, some are just noise. What to do? Signals, or signs from our future, are nothing more than potential disruptors. Because disruptors follow the universal impact pattern, it is quite easy to distinguish between noise and the signals that matter.

> **Key Thought: Signals are potential disruptors.**

The challenge lies in evaluating the signal's potential in creating behavior space relevant to our situation.

Compounding the problem is the fact that not all disruptors are equal in their impacts. Compare the behavior space impacts of electricity and the pencil. The pencil, a simple object, allows us to write anywhere, including upside down. While it's a valuable addition to our behavior universe, it pales in comparison to electricity. Think of all the items powered by electricity. Now, think of all the behaviors we do with those items. Electricity's behavior space is massive. We depend on it for everyday tasks. The pencil is an object with limited behavior space potential. It cannot grow past its own potential. Electricity is a platform that powers other disruptors. Its behavior space potential grows as each new device (vacuum cleaner, lights, ovens) is created.

> **Key thought: the power of a disruptor is determined by how much behavior space it can create. Platform disruptors' behavior space potential grows as new devices are created.**

A TOOL TO ASSESS SIGNALS

With this distinguishing characteristic in mind, we can now construct a signal analyzer.

We've included a signal analyzer tool in Figure 2. This tool uses the universal pattern. In using the tool, you use the pattern, and when you use the pattern, two new behaviors emerge for you:

1. You filter signals through a universal pattern, independent of your experience and industry. In doing so, you will understand signals that previously had no meaning for you.
2. Because you now understand these signals, you can apply an analysis of the relevant ones to your situation. In doing so, you see opportunities to which you were previously blind.

Signal Analyzing

To assess a signal's potential, you need to accomplish four tasks:

1. Assess whether a signal is relevant or noise.
2. Assess the signal's behavior space impact in the originating environment.
3. Imagine how that behavior space impact would be useful in your environment.
4. Assess your capacity to implement the disruptor.

Signal or Noise

To determine whether a signal is relevant or noise, ask the following questions:

1. What is the scope of the behavioral impact? How large was the impact in the originating environment? How significant an impact would it make in your environment?
2. Can you think of an application of the new behavior in your environment? How would it benefit those who adopted the new behavior?

Noise: The British royal wedding in 2011 was watched by millions of people around the world. What did it signify? From a behavioral standpoint, ladies' hats became more popular. There was a shift of purchases toward these hats. Did a new behavior space emerge? No. Perhaps there was for people who had previously never considered wearing hats. But overall, the impact was small and unsustainable. It was entertainment, not value creation. The wedding, as popular as it was, was simply noise. People's habits did not change.

Key Thought: Disruptors cause new habits to form.

Figure 2: The Signal Analyzer[9]

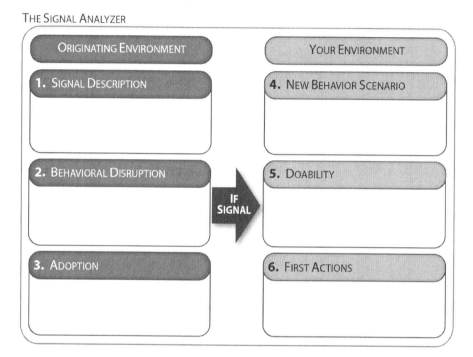

THE SIGNAL ANALYZER

ORIGINATING ENVIRONMENT

1. SIGNAL DESCRIPTION

2. BEHAVIORAL DISRUPTION

IF SIGNAL

3. ADOPTION

YOUR ENVIRONMENT

4. NEW BEHAVIOR SCENARIO

5. DOABILITY

6. FIRST ACTIONS

Instructions

Signals are information about emerging new behaviors occurring outside your normal frame of reference. Now that you understand that the root of all disruptors and signals lies in expanding behavior space, you can assess their value in your environment.

Originating Environment

First, analyze the signal or disruptor in its originating environment by asking the following questions:

1. What is the new disruptor? An idea, a technology, a platform? Use this portion to keep track of where the signal came from so you can communicate it to others.
2. What changes in behavior does the disruptor cause? There are four kinds of behavior change to watch for:
   o Eliminated behaviors
   o Enhanced behaviors
   o Reduced behaviors
   o Added behaviors (Think of the phone call, bike riding, or tweeting.)
   How significant is the adoption of this behavior? Is usage pervasive and growing? How deep and pervasive is the language used to describe the item and its usage?

> **Key Thought: Signals and the disruptors they represent change behavior in four ways: Eliminate, Enhance, Reduce, and Add.**

Your Environment

Then, given that the signal has significant impact, assess its potential in your environment by taking the following three steps:

1. Transport the emerging behavior to your environment. How could you use that behavior in your world? What behaviors could you eliminate, enhance, reduce, or add? What benefits would this behavioral disruption provide?

2. What will you need to learn to make this disruptor work in your environment? What new capabilities or processes will need to be put in place? How will you adapt the disruptor to your environment?[10]
3. What are the first actions you will take to test this idea?

A Signal Sample

3-D printing, one of the exponential technologies discussed in the prologue, provides an interesting case study. On November 24, 2012, *The Economist*[11] reported that GE Aviation had acquired Morris Technologies of Cincinnati Ohio for its 3-D technologies.

Let's deal with just that one signal and see how we might transport it to a design and research company by using the signal interpreter. I chose the research company because it does not seem related to jet engine manufacturing.

Originating Environment

Step 1: Signal Description

Here's what *The Economist* had to say:

> Among the 3-D printing technologies used by Morris Technologies is laser sintering. This involves spreading a thin layer of metallic powder onto a build platform and then fusing the material with a laser beam. The process is repeated until an object emerges. Laser sintering is capable of producing all kinds of metal parts, including components made from aerospace-grade titanium.[12]

Step 2: Behavior Disruption

Manufacturing is a wasteful process. Waste is created when parts fabricated from materials have pieces cut away. To achieve economies of scale, we traditionally manufacture identical parts. This mass manufacturing process reduces parts waste as well as the waste of labor involved in setting up machines. However, substantial waste still remains.

3-D printing completely eliminates both of those forms of waste. Operators don't need to operate machines, nor do they spend the time required to set them up. Parts are made directly from the 3-D drawings, consuming only the raw materials used in the process.

Here are two quotes from the *Economist* article that signal what the new behavior space that 3-D printing brings:

> Many manufacturers already use 3-D printing to make prototypes of parts, because it is cheaper and more flexible than tooling up to produce just one or two items.

> Designs can be quickly changed, so the technology enables flexible production and mass customization.[13]

Step 3: Adoption

GE Aviation just made a purchase of a one hundred thirty-person firm because it can "see the purchase as an investment in an important new manufacturing technology." According to Colleen Athans, general manager of GE Aviation's supply-chain operations, "Our ability to develop state of the art manufacturing processes for emerging materials and complex design geometry is critical to our future."[14]

This statement sends a strong signal of the disruptive power of 3-D printing. When we consider that GE Aviation is using it for aviation parts, we can safely conclude that 3-D printing is not noise, it's real.

Your Environment

Now that we've understood GE Aviation and their use of 3-D printing, what can we do with it in a research and design firm?

Step 4: New Behavior Scenario

Here's a new behavior space for the design and research firm.

The firm works with clients that make tangible products. The research firm develops a user-friendly CAD interface that allows their clients' customers to modify the design of a product. Imagine a situation where these customers' users interact with a number of preprinted prototypes, make changes to the CAD designs, and then new proto-types are printed. The cycle is repeated until the customers develop their own version of a desired item.

The research company has now created an interactive, live process where customers interactively engage with tangible objects and their design to influence the final product.

Here are examples of how they could eliminate, enhance, reduce, and add behaviors:

1. Reduce the time required between meetings about different prototype reviews with users.
2. Eliminate paper concept reviews and go straight to prototype reviews.

3. Enhance users' interaction with the devices by having multiple prototypes available.
4. Add the ability for users to input directly into the design stage.

It would change the nature of the relationship between not only the customers and the client sponsor, but between the research company and the client as well. Now the design and research firm designs products for their clients using direct input from their clients' customers. Without 3-D printing, this high level of engagement with users is not economically feasible.

Step 5: Doability

The company will need to figure out how to:

1. Develop the user interface.
2. Determine what kind of printer and raw materials to use based on client product designs.
3. Modify its research process and revenue model to include the enhanced client customer-engagement process.

Step 6: First Actions

Here are some first actions the company could take over the next sixty days:

1. Research client product designs, including their existing process and costs of materials used.
2. Research the types and costs of 3-D printers available.
3. Develop a concept illustration highlighting the process and benefits of 3D printing.
4. Test the concept illustration with favored clients.

Signal or Noise?

A signal is noise when one or both of two conditions are met:

1. The behavior change in the originating environment is small.
2. You cannot determine a relevant application of the technology or a change in the behavior space of your environment.

Insights into Behavior Disruption

Let's examine the GE Aviation example in more detail.

The *elimination of waste* is a good example of eliminating a behavior. By saving those resources, the company can deploy the savings in materials costs and labor elsewhere.

Quick prototyping is a good example of an enhanced behavior. Likely, GE Aviation would have created prototypes before, but not at the speed and volume allowed by 3-D printing. It's probable, given the waste savings, that 3-D printing allows GE Aviation to create multiple prototypes in the same amount of time and for the same cost as it took to create a single one previously.

Reducing the number times that GE must tool up to create one or two copies is a good example of a reduced behavior.

Mass customization is a good example of an added behavior. It also creates a new terminology combining the word *mass* from *mass production* with *customization*. In the summer of 2013, GE held an online contest for contestants to take an existing metal jet engine loading bracket and reimagine it for 3-D metal printing manufacturing. GE wanted the bracket to achieve a lighter weight, but still maintain its strength. The winner's submission reduced the bracket's overall weight by 84 percent while still maintaining the strength requirements necessary for real-world conditions.

You adopt a new signal to improve the current state of your business through the elimination, reduction, and enhancement of behaviors. Those behavior changes make you better than your competitors. However, you make your biggest leap to leadership by doing something no one else can do. That capability comes from the *added* behavior that did not exist before you brought it to market.

For GE Aviation, it will be better than its competitors because it eliminates waste and can do quicker, cost-effective prototyping. However it will be *different* when it can customize engines in ways no one else can.

> **Key Thought: Not all behavior space changes are equal. Eliminating, enhancing, and reducing behaviors make you better. Adding new behaviors makes you different.**

Conclusions for Disruptive Leaders

1. Signals are only as powerful as the behavior change they portend. Little change, little power. Watch the big ones that change behavior dramatically, often by eliminating jobs.
2. Signals are only as relevant as the value of the behavior change transported to your customers' environment. Know your customers' existing behavioral norm as it relates to you and your competitors' offerings. That norm is what you seek to disrupt.
3. Watching and interpreting signals outside your business's frame of reference is the new core competency. Without it, you are blind and can only react.
4. As a disruptive leader, recalibrate how your organization listens so that you see the signs from the future before others.

Exercise: Signal behavior watching

1. Watch customers use your offering. List the behaviors your offering provides. What capabilities do they now have that they previously did not?
2. Learn about one of the twelve technologies listed above.
3. Use the *Signal Analyzer* to extract the new behaviors this technology enables.
4. Apply these new behaviors to your customers' use of your offering. How would the new behavior make life better for them?

Chapter 3: The Chunky Future

OVERVIEW

I've described how disruption follows a universal pattern and how, in using the pattern, we can uncover the signs from the future to become a disruptive leader. Our next question to answer is "How are barriers to entry created?"

We measure the future in the same way that we measure the past: by days, months, years, and decades. Unfortunately, that all-pervasive view of how we perceive the future is counterproductive. When it comes to seeing the opportunities signals represent, you need to throw out time as your filter and replace it with *uncertainty*.

A STORY ILLUSTRATING HOW THE FUTURE BECOMES THE PRESENT

In 1865, Jules Verne published a fantasy novel called *From the Earth to the Moon*. So began the Space Race that ended on July 16, 1969 with Neil Armstrong's famous words, "That's one small step for [a] man, one giant leap for mankind."

The history of that race, which in 1865 was never recognized as one, illustrates how our behavior toward signals can turn fantasy into reality. In this next section you'll learn how the future:

- Contains "chunky" time periods based on their levels of uncertainty
- Accelerates the transformation of future-based ideas into tangible items based on resource commitments, three roles played, and desire
- Provides the best opportunity to create differentiation barriers

For decades after the publication of Verne's book, travel to the moon remained a fantasy. Jules Verne proposed using a cannon to enable a moon shot. Surprisingly, some of his calculations about the requirements of the cannon were quite accurate. By 1905, while the idea still remained a fantasy, serious work had been done.

Konstantin Tsiolkovsky, a Russian rocket scientist, developed a theory of jet propulsion in 1887. In 1903, he published a technical article that accurately predicted the horizontal speed required for a minimal orbit and how this speed could be achieved by means of a multistage rocket fueled by liquid oxygen and hydrogen.[15] Finally, he refuted Verne's idea of using a cannon for space travel by demonstrating how the gun would have to be impossibly long.

In the 1920s, Robert Goddard built the first liquid-fueled rockets, the first of which flew on March 16, 1926. Between 1926 and 1941, his rockets achieved altitudes as high as 2.6 km.[16] Others followed his lead.

In February of 1935, Nazi Germany established its missile program to explore the viability of rocket-based weapons. In 1942, Germany launched the first rocket into outer space, the A4. Rocket technology that could reach the moon hadn't been proved, but a solution to how one could travel was now in sight.

Fast-forward to the late 1950s. The Soviet Union and the United States were locked in a battle to prove whose system of governance was superior. Space travel was a key battlefield.

In 1955, within a period of just four days, both nations publicly announced that they would launch artificial earth satellites by 1958 (the International Geophysical Year).[17] So began what became known as the *Space Race*.

On October 4, 1957, the Soviets successfully launched Sputnik, the world's first artificial satellite, into orbit. The United States responded with Explorer 1 on January 31, 1958. On July 29 of the same year, President Eisenhower created NASA to take over earlier rocket programs with a budget of $100 million. Eisenhower then followed that up by committing to the Apollo program, and three-man space flight, in 1960.

While there were discussions about landing a man on the moon in the scenarios explored, there still remained no specific goal to do so. That changed in April 1961. Until then, the Soviets and the Americans had only committed to a race to put a man in space. On April 12th, the USSR launched cosmonaut Yuri Gagarin into orbit. President Kennedy was not pleased, to say the least. Eight days after Gagarin's flight, Kennedy sent a memo to Vice President Lyndon B. Johnson, asking him to look into the state of America's space program and what might offer NASA the opportunity to catch up.

Johnson responded ten days later, where he recommended that a piloted moon landing was far enough in the future that it was likely the United States could achieve it first.

Finally, twenty days later, on May 25, in a special joint session of Congress, Kennedy announced his support for the Apollo program and redefined the ultimate goal of the Space Race, "I believe that this nation should commit itself to achieving the goal, before this decade is out, of landing a man on the moon and returning him safely to the Earth."[18]

A little over eight years later, the race was over and a man was on the moon. Traveling to the moon was now a reality.

What started as a fantasy turned into a possibility, and finally, a reality.

This story showcases how people imagine a fantastically impossible future and turn it into reality. Signals play the role of signs from the future alerting us to the enormous possibilities they portend.

To understand how signals work together, and how best to exploit them, we must first see the future as it really exists, in chunks.

The Future is chance that arrives in chunks

We live in an age in which we know that the future will be different from the present. That wasn't always so. For most of mankind's history, life was very static. Only hundreds of years ago, most of the human population lived as peasants working the land. They were born into their station in life, worked as countless generations before them had, and died in their station. Change happened slowly, over generations, so slowly it often was not noticed. The future was the same as the present and the same as the past. People came and people went. Nothing really changed.

That's not true today. We expect the world to change, not just over generations, but within a generation. We expect the future to be different than the present. We don't just expect it, we *know* the future will be different!

That begs the following questions: "How is a different, a changed future, made? If there are an infinitive number of possible futures, why are we living in the one we are living in now? How does that happen?"

What is the Future?

Most people, when thinking about the future, think about time. Unfortunately, when it comes to signals, that approach blinds us to rich opportunities.

Fact 1: The future flows toward us.

We live in the present. As we live and breathe, time passes by, and the future arrives. Here's what that means: reading those last three sentences took about five seconds. When you started reading those sentences, the end of the third sentence was five seconds in your future. By the time you finished reading it, that future, previously five seconds away, was in your present. And by now, it is about ten seconds in your past.

Clear? As time passes by, the future flows toward us.

Fact 2: Our life and business trajectories are mostly stable.

During the time you were reading those sentences, your life did not change dramatically. Who you love, your finances, your career trajectory, and the other things important to you stayed on course. So while the future was flowing toward you, its impact on your life, business, and all your relationships was negligible. In that regard, your present, your near-past, and your near-future are all the same. They have little to no impact on your trajectory (catastrophes and business disruptions aside).[19]

Normally, we think of time as flowing past us smoothly, much like the graphic below, in which we sit in the now and the future moves toward us.

Figure 3. Now

However, when we consider the flow of time and its impact on the trajectory of our lives and businesses, it behaves more like the next graphic, in which the past, present, and future are all part of the now. What I call the *knowable future* is the time between now and a point in the future where uncertainty is completely known or knowable.

It is time in which we are quite certain about where we have come from and where we are going. From an impact perspective, nothing much has changed in the past five seconds, minutes, hours, days, weeks, or months, and nothing much will change in the next five seconds, minutes, hours, days, weeks, or months either.

Figure 4. The Knowable Now

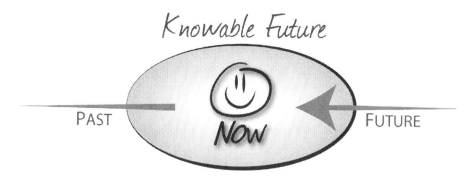

While time does flow smoothly by, its impact on our lives passes by in chunks. This explains why all societies have created ceremonies to delineate the movement from one chunk to another: childhood to adulthood, single to married, living to dead. It's a cultural recognition that the impact of time is experienced in chunks, not smoothly. We celebrate each movement into a new chunk.

> ### Key Thought: We experience life in chunks.

We know the past, we know the now, and for a certain period of time, we can know the future too. In fact, we spend much of our lives trying to make the future knowable. That's one reason why businesses go through annual planning cycles—to take future events and put them into the knowable future by giving them more certainty.

However, at some point, we do reach a time where we don't feel that our core issues and opportunities are knowable. Our projections are just too unreliable. Therefore, the length of time between now and that critical uncertainty point in our future represents our knowable future. Anything past that future point and we don't feel comfortable that we can reliably predict our trajectory. However, not all things in our lives have the same time frame of knowability. For example, when we are out of work, the time when we will find work is unknowable. We are living in uncertainty. Conversely, the duration of our marriage could be quite knowable. Our future, as we normally conceive of it, as being unknowable, actually lies at a point of time that varies by the topic's knowability.

> ### Key Thought: The future is best understood by grouping it by its knowability.

So, from a practical standpoint, our future is divided into aspects of our lives that are quite knowable for a substantial period of time, and other aspects that are not knowable.

Figure 5. The Unknowable Future

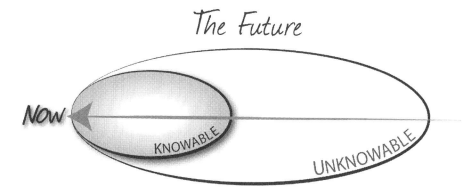

However, the future doesn't transition abruptly from completely knowable to completely unknowable. Two other stages of the future exist between now and the unknowable future. It's in these two areas, between the knowable and the unknowable future, where barriers to entry are created.

The landing of men on the moon and all other inventions, innovations, and disruptive changes were created in these two stages between the knowable now and the unknowable future.

The Future We Experience Starts with Dreamers

There are an infinite number of futures that await us. The future we live through starts with dreamers, artisans, and other creative types. They dream and imagine. Jules Verne was not the only person who thought about man travelling to the moon. But he was the one who popularized it. When he published his book, he created the question in people's minds: "How can we travel to the moon?" It didn't cost him much to imagine and publish his idea. Likely, he made money doing it.

His idea of traveling to the moon by cannon shot came from nothing. He simply imagined it. He created, from the infinite possibilities of the unknowable future one idea and popularized it. In so doing, he created an imaginary future, a fantastic one for his time, but a *different future* than existed before. His book disrupted how people thought about the future by adding a new idea of what it might look like. His book acted as a signal from the future: *we will travel to the moon.* His idea of moon travel populated a portion of the future called the *imagined future,* namely, the point in the future where fantastic ideas reside, where uncertainty is high but not infinite. We don't know *when* it will occur. We just know it *might* occur.

> **Key Thought: Dreamers populate the imagined future with imaginary, impossible ideas.**

However, more than just creating an idea, his book achieved something else that was equally important.

His book created an uncertainty space, a series of implied questions to be answered to make the imagined future a reality. "How can we travel to the moon? What do we need to know? What do we need to do to achieve this goal?" are all questions his book prompted. Obviously in the mid-1800s no one had any idea of the millions of questions that would need to be answered. That's not important. What's important is that people use the idea to uncover the limited number[20] of relevant questions that need to be answered. This leads us to the second phenomenon of the imagined future. Ideas in the imagined future attract others to uncover all the relevant questions that need answering.[21] That's true of all ideas in the imagined future. They attract people to explore whatever is needed to make the future happen. Remember *Star Trek* in the 1960s? The show prominently featured several devices such as mobile memory and cell phones. These were fantasies, like Verne's, if not quite so distant in becoming realities. That's how the future happens. Someone creates a fantastic idea. That idea attracts others to discover the questions that need to be answered and to solve them. This is what I call the *uncertainty framework*, or the questions that need to be discovered and answered to make that future real.

That's what dreamers do. They create ideas of the future that populate our imaginations and provide a framework for their exploration and development.

> **Key Thought: The imagined future provides the impetus for innovation by creating an uncertainty framework that attracts others to experiment.**

Figure 6. The Imaginary Future

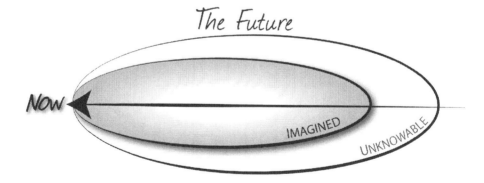

Inventors Take Over

As the popularity of Verne's book spread, he stimulated other people to think about his idea and explore it. For Verne, his work was done. He was a dreamer. He made his living by dreaming and populating the present with new ideas about the future. He left it to others to explore and tinker with them. And they did.

During this time of the imaginary future,[22] inventors developed useful technologies. In 1896, Konstantin Tsiolkovsky discovered the mathematical formulas used in designing liquid-fueled rocket propulsion. In the 1920s, Robert Goddard invented the first liquid-fueled rockets. The Germans continued rocket development in the 1930s and achieved the first outer space launch in the mid-1940s. None of these inventors were trying to travel to the moon. They focused on present day applications of the idea. Nonetheless, they were laying the groundwork for the moon shot. In the same way, Sir Isaac Newton unknowingly laid the groundwork for moon travel with his development of calculus in the late 1700s.

That's the role inventors play. They tinker with ideas by running experiments and building prototypes. Each effort transforms a piece of the uncertainty into certainty: We do it *this* way, not *that* way. It works *this* way, not *that* way. Inventors strip away the uncertainty of an imagined future one experiment and prototype at a time until there remain no more unknown uncertainties to be found. Along the way, they uncover new uncertainties that were previously hidden to them. They add these new uncertainties to the list and go to work on them. Over time, they discover the entire uncertainty framework needed to turn an idea into a reality.

Once the entire uncertainty framework is uncovered, the idea moves out of the imagined future into the *possible future*. Uncovering the entire uncertainty framework does not imply that all the questions have been answered. It only means that we know all the relevant questions to be answered. An idea stops being imaginary and becomes possible when all uncertainties are known, but not necessarily resolved.

> **Key Thought: Inventors work in the imagined future prototyping an impossible idea into a possible one.**

Figure 7. The Possible Future

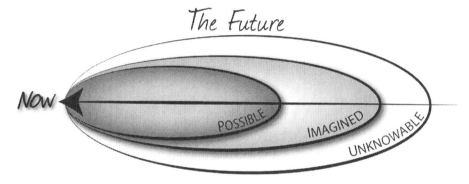

In the case of the moon shot, there were many categories of uncertainties that needed to be answered, each one a critical step on the journey. The illustration at the end of this chunk highlights four of those categories.

1. How do we send a rocket to outer space?
2. How do we orbit the Earth?
3. How do we send a man to space and back safely?
4. How do we send men to the moon and back safely?

> **Key Thought: Inventors run their experiments on supporting ideas that provide immediate returns.**

Mind you, dreamers don't suddenly disappear. They continue to play a supporting role by keeping the idea alive and popular. For instance, H.G. Wells published *The First Men on the Moon* in 1901. A year later, the Méliès brothers produced a fourteen-minute silent film, *A Trip to the Moon*. In 1958, RKO Pictures released a film adaptation of Jules Verne's original book, *From the Earth to the Moon*. All of these dreamers kept Verne's original idea of moon travel alive in the twentieth century.

> **Key thought: an imagined future becomes possible when we know what we don't know and a working prototype is made.**

The moon landing moved into the possible future in the late 1950s when the Soviet Union and the United States announced their intentions to put human beings into space. By *possible future*, I mean that point in the future when all uncertainties are known and a prototype is made. By then, the uncertainty framework had been identified: propulsion, telemetry, human protection, and so on. What was missing to move it through the possible future into a reality was the *desire* to go to the moon.

Entrepreneurs Make It Real

Once an idea moves out of the imagined future into the possible future, entrepreneurs step in and turn the possible future into the present. Inventors create the possible future and then work with entrepreneurs to make it real. But it's not preordained that entrepreneurs will take on an idea. That takes desire.

The possible future that became reality when Apollo 11 reached the moon started in the late 1950s, when the governments of the Soviet

Union and the United States announced and funded the Space Race. We don't often think of governments as entrepreneurs, but that's the role they played in this case. These government entrepreneurs did what all entrepreneurs do. They took a possibility and organized it, funded it, and, importantly, possessed the desire to make it real.

> **Key thought: Entrepreneurs organize the possible into something real.**

For each of the stages, putting a rocket in outer space, having it orbit the Earth, having human beings orbit the Earth, and achieving a moon landing, moved the future from possible to real. Each stage, on the day of its achievement, became part of here and now. Most importantly, it became knowable. As we will see in the next section, things knowable by some people often remain in the future (and unknowable) for others.

It was not preordained that the United States would land a man on the moon, nor that they would do so by the end of 1960s. That was never the intent of the announcement made by Eisenhower during his term, nor the ones made by Kennedy during the 1960 elections. Up until early 1961, the two presidents had committed to funding satellites and putting men in space. Neither had committed to the resources required to put a man on the moon. It was the May 25, 1961 speech to Congress that committed the United States to landing on the moon. Those resources were committed because the Soviet Union had launched a man into space three weeks before the United States. Three weeks made all the difference.

> **Key thought: Desire drives the resources required to move an idea from the imagined future to the now.**

Imagine what might have happened if the Soviet Union had put a man into space after the United States. It's unlikely that Neil Armstrong would have landed on the moon in July of 1969. It's possible that mankind never would have gone to the moon at all. Had it been different, the idea of putting men on the moon might still exist only in the *possible future* today, waiting for an entrepreneur with enough desire to move it forward.

Figure 8. The Complete Uncertainty Future

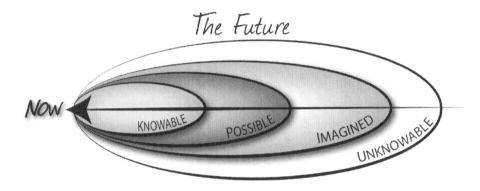

Summary

> **Key thought: First we dream. Then we invent. Then we organize.**

Earlier, I said that the future flows steadily toward us. From the perspective of time, that's true. However, from the perspective of what the future will be like, that's not true. The future is chunky and not preordained. Dreamers, inventors, and entrepreneurs *make* the future we will live in. Each has an important role to play.

Dreamers start the process by creating a fantastic idea for how the world will behave. The TV show *Star Trek* in the 1960s created the vision of a world in which we communicate with little handheld devices and travel by warp drive.[23] Jules Verne created the idea of traveling to the moon. On the day his book was published, the idea of travel to the moon moved from the unknowable future to the imagined future.

The human species is innately curious. We are hardwired to explore. New and fantastic ideas unleash the desires of the explorer in us, specifically for inventors who love to figure out how to do the impossible. These ideas populated in an imagined future by the dreamer provide the uncertainty framework for inventors to explore. Inventors then do what they love best, expanding the unknowns, discovering new methods and technologies, and resolving the problems and barriers needed to achieve a vision. During this time of invention, a vast number of details are uncovered and discovered. The knowledge of those details, what works, what doesn't, and why, represents an equally vast array of barriers to entry. They are turned into patents, trade secrets, or locked-in relationships. These inventions create the barriers to entry companies covet.

For example, Apple does a remarkable job of locking in relationships with suppliers that have invented proprietary technologies and manufacturing techniques for them. Competitors can't compete because they don't have access to these secret tools, methods, or technologies. The idea of travel to the moon stayed in the imagined future for almost a century while inventors experimented and turned the idea into various prototypes, some successful, most not.

During the invention stage, the greatest barriers are erected. The "trade secret effect" accounts for why German rocket scientists from World War II populated both the Soviet and US missile programs in the 1950s. Both countries needed the scientists in order to obtain the secrets of rocket flight and control. Duplicating their work would have set them back by years.

Finally, inventors reach a point in their experimentation where so much is understood about what it takes, or will take, that the idea moves from an imaginary one to a possible one, or from the imagined future to the possible future. That's when entrepreneurs with desire become heavily involved, applying their skills of acquiring funding, organizing, and expanding markets. By becoming involved at this transition phase, entrepreneurs become potential owners of the secrets, just as the Soviet and US governments became owners of the missile secrets of German scientists.

Finally, when an idea becomes possible, the amount of money allocated accelerates. In the case of the Space Race, when entrepreneurs took over in the late 1950s, the initial funding started at $100 million, the amount committed by President Eisenhower for the creation of NASA. The final cost of just the Apollo program was reported to Congress in 1973 as $25.4 billion, or $109 billion in 2010 terms.

Entities involved in this transition from the possible future to the here and now have a chance to own a portion of those invention barriers. Those that wait until the idea arrives in the here and now don't.

> **Key thought: The greatest barriers to entry are created during the Imagined and possible Futures. Those who participate reap the rewards of those barriers. Those who wait until the here and now are locked out.**

Figure 9. The Uncertainty Stages of the Moon Landing

HOW THE FUTURE IS MADE
From the earth to the moon

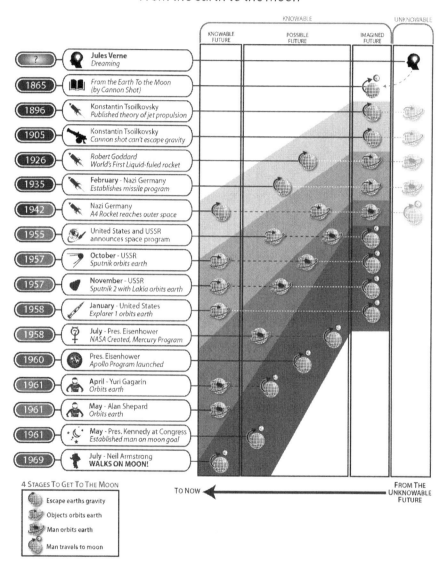

Conclusions For the Disruptive Leader

1. While we experience life through time, we make our lives real by resolving uncertainty.
2. The future we will live in five years from now will be made by those leaders who choose to engage with and resolve the uncertainties associated with what was once just a dream.
3. As a disruptive leader, recalibrate thinking in the organization to focus on what it doesn't know, as well as what it knows. Resolving those uncertainties rather than pushing them aside will provide the greatest opportunities.

Exercise: Evaluate your capacity

1. Take stock of your employees and suppliers.
   - Who are the natural dreamers?
   - Who are the natural inventors?
   - Who are the natural entrepreneurs?
2. What management systems do you have in place where these people can create and implement future scenarios that are not just extensions of the past?
3. How do these scenarios fit into your strategic planning process?

Chapter 4: Go Where The Future Is

INTRODUCTION

For many people, the future happens and they react to it. They spend their lives trying to make the best of things as they can. Millions of business owners behave this way too. They react to the events in their industry and fight a never-ending battle to keep from being commoditized. You can see it in their eyes and in what they say. "It's a constant battle. How do I stay on top? Margins are down. It's becoming harder every year to compete." They look for faster ways to react, for the latest thing that everyone talks about.

Unfortunately, their fundamental premise is false. Success is not about being better at reacting. The future does not happen. The future is made by dreamers, inventors and entrepreneurs. Mankind was not destined to go to the moon, drive cars, or live in heated houses. None of these or the millions of other inventions that make our lives what they are today were preordained. Humans made the future! That implies we have a choice. We can live our lives reacting to the future or we can choose to make it. Whether made knowingly or not, that choice is the greatest, most profound strategic decision organizations make.

> **Key Thought: The single most important strategic choice is whether to react to the future or make it.**

CREATING INTELLECTUAL PROPERTY AND BARRIERS TO ENTRY

If you choose to *make* your future, then you have to work *in* the future. That means you need to be involved in the invention process. You can't make the future by copying the ideas and technologies available in the present. You must see past what is available now and work in the possible and imagined futures. That's what the *Man to the Moon* story told us. One hundred and four years passed between the publication of Jules Verne's book in 1865 and Neil Armstrong's moonwalk. For most of that time, traveling to the moon was imaginary, a dream for poets and filmmakers. It wasn't until the 1950s that it became possible, and not until 1961, because of happenstance, that a firm goal was established to make it happen. To this day, only one country has sent men to the moon. So while the space technology exists today, travel to the moon still resides in the knowable future for all other countries in the world. It's technically feasible, but it remains in their futures.[24]

Those companies that participated in the invention stage during the imagined future had the potential to share in the benefits associated with the barriers created by the uncertainty platform. For example, one of the most difficult challenges they overcame was the development of a rocket booster able to place a payload of twenty to forty thousand pounds into earth orbit. Rocketdyne was the company that invented the Saturn V rocket originally specified by Wernher von Braun, one of the original German rocket scientists of the 1930s. The company was founded in 1955 in Canoga Park, California. It went through several mergers. Even today, Rocketdyne, now a part of Boeing, remains the premier rocket engine design and production company in the United States. That's what happens to companies that don't work with known technology, but instead invent the future.

But it is not in just massive projects like moon travel where barriers to entry can be seen. They occur every day. Facebook launched in 2005 and grew rapidly to become the world's largest social networking site. Apple launched its iTunes store in April of 2003 and the App Store in the fall of 2007. Both of these platforms created significant barriers to entry behind them.

Today there are millions of companies that do not have a presence on Facebook. Facebook is here now. But for those that haven't participated, Facebook remains in the future. I'm not arguing for everyone to go on Facebook. Business owners need to believe there are compelling reasons to do so. Instead, I'm making the following two points:

1. A technology[25] can be in the now to some people but still in *your* future.
2. Working in the now offers very little differentiation advantage.

> **Key thought: Each entity has its own personal future.**
> **What's in your now may be in my knowable future.**

Let's say a small consulting company creates a presence on Facebook. It develops a community and gains more satisfied customers. Luckily for the company, it is the only one in its local market area to do so. But what's to stop its competitors from doing the same thing? What can the first company learn that the competition can't? Nothing. That's the problem in working with technologies in the now. It's very hard to create barriers to entry behind you.[26] Differentiation is not just about how different and valuable you are. It's equally about how well you can sustain that differentiation by constructing barriers to entry. Working in the now provides only transient advantages. The advantage gained doesn't last.

> **Key thought: Differentiation strength equals the relative value of your competitive differences times the strength of barriers to entry.**

Let's compare a couple of stories to see what I mean.

You'd have to be living in a cave not to be aware of the launch of the iPad on January 27, 2010. Apple launched a big marketing campaign prior to the first deliveries, as only they can. Steve Jobs performed onstage followed by massive press coverage.

A simple question to ask ourselves is, "How many people in your company *did not know* about the iPad on the day it was launched?" Was there even one? Everyone sensed the iPad. They knew about it, and to a greater or lesser extent had evaluated it.

Prior to the launch, the capabilities of the iPad, its position in the computing market, and its functionality were largely unknown. We knew something was coming, likely a tablet, and it was a reasonable guess that it would utilize the iOS that runs the iPhone. That knowledge resided in the possible future. All that changed on the day of the launch. Its capabilities, usability, and functionality became part of the now. Of course, on the day of the launch, we didn't know the exact characteristics of all the apps that would be made. But given that we knew of the apps produced for the iPhone, we could make intelligent guesses. The iPad capabilities were mostly knowable.

You could commercialize the iPad on the day it was announced. At that point, if a business were thinking about using it to gain a competitive edge, they were too late. Why? On the day of the launch, all your competitors had access to the same information. You may not have known it, but it was available and therefore was knowable.

Your competitors could learn the same techniques and imagine the same kinds of uses. There was no inherent advantage. It simply became a race of the fastest. Any market leadership gained only lasts until the competition catches up. Building differentiation based on existing technologies is classic reacting.

> **Key Thought: Adopting technologies available today offers few sustainable barriers to entry as the technology is knowable to everyone.**

That is not to say that no one did anything spectacular with the iPad. American Airlines adopted them for pilot manuals in the cockpit. By reducing the weight from the thirty-eight pounds of pilot flight documents to the one-and-a-half pound iPad, they expect to save one million dollars a year in fuel costs alone. iPads are also transforming education delivery and medical record keeping. But while these examples provide strong advantages for the adopters, those advantages won't last.

Think of it this way: Facebook, iPad apps, smartphone apps, Twitter, industrial robotics, and many others, are all here now. Perhaps no one in your industry is using one of these technologies. Great, if you're the first to adopt one, then you can create a competitive advantage, such as better customer service. But the advantage it creates for you will only last as long as the time it takes for your competitors to copy it or improve upon it. That's what most organizations do. They look out to see what's available now and adopt it to their operations. Someone else invents it and they adopt it. For those adopters, it's a race to see who can learn the fastest.

The big winners in these stories are Facebook and Apple. They own the platforms that everyone else adopts. They own a piece of the app revenue that the platforms generate. That's who the winners are, the platform owners, the Microsofts, the Apples, the Facebooks, the Googles.

But that has been true for all technologies. Remember the touch-tone phone, the electric typewriter,[27] the fax machine, the IBM PC computer, and the Internet? They all were disruptive in their day. They have all been adopted and some were subsequently discarded. Did they provide an advantage to those adopters, especially the early ones? Yes. Did that advantage last? No. Over time, they simply became the price of entry.

Now, compare the iPad story to the solar-powered contact lens created by Professor Babak Parviz at the University of Washington. Its launch was published in 2009. No fanfare. No glitz.

On April 2010, *Fast Company*[28] magazine published an article about a solar-powered contact lens that would disrupt our business lives. It would augment vision, be used as a remote control or sensing device, and later versions might even display text or take pictures. So how many people in your company know about the solar-powered contact lens? Was there even one? If not, then no one sensed this nascent technology. It is not broadly known, even now, four years later.

That's because the solar-powered contact lens is still in the imagined future. As of September 2013, there was not even a fully functioning prototype, although they have been tested for wearability. It needs entrepreneurs to take an idea to market with specific business applications. That's where you could play a role. That means if you were to engage with Professor Parviz now, you would have a chance to influence how it comes to market. You could shape the technology in various ways, depending on your industry. Here are some examples:

1. Financial traders on the stock exchanges will use it to see the trajectory of trades they are following.
2. Pilots will use it to keep their eyes outside the window.
3. Police officers will use it, along with facial recognition, to identify who is in the car when they approach.
4. Surgeons will use it to see updates on the status of their patients without diverting their attention from the patient.
5. Real estate agents will use it to see comparisons of the house they are showing clients with recent real-time sale prices in the area.
6. Repair people will use it to identify parts on an object they are repairing that are new to them.
7. Retailers will use it to look at items on the shelf and determine the brands and sizes that are moving with the greatest velocity that day.
8. Landscapers will use it to identify grubs in the lawn to apply the correct insecticide.
9. Politicians will use it to identify the big campaign contributors in a crowd.

If you are a large company with significant resources, you could make investments to own a piece of the technology.[29] If you are a smaller company, you could work with them to build the user interface platform that feeds specific applications. You could then license it to users.

For example, as part of a medical company, you could design how best to flow information across the contact lens used by surgeons. You could own that part of the technology,[30] allowing you to become a platform player in the same way that Apple is the platform owner with its App Store.

So, working with the professor to develop a working prototype that your company could use would not only give you a leap ahead of the competition, it would also create barriers to entry. Working with something in the early stages means that you run across technical, legal, and other issues that need to be resolved. Resolving those issues, issues that at first only you know about, becomes the barrier to entry for competitors. Doing so creates the potential for disruptive offerings with greater sustainability.

Here's another example of how to reach out and claim a piece of the future for your own.

The Rogers Research Group[31] is a part of the University of Illinois. As they say on their home page:

> We seek to understand and exploit interesting characteristics of 'soft' materials, such as polymers, liquid crystals, and biological tissues as well as hybrid combinations of them with unusual classes of micro/nanomaterials, in the form of ribbons, wires, membranes, tubes or related materials.[32]

Sounds both confusing and interesting. A further exploration shows videos of the applications on which they are working. These applications include epidural electronics, with devices that are as light and unobtrusive as the patch tattoos children buy. Other applications they show include: monitoring health indicators such as electrocardiograms and epileptic seizures, controlling robotic helicopters with hand gestures, and wearable, stretchable lithium batteries to power other devices.

These applications suggest enormous disruptive power. Here are three examples of the disruptions that are possible in very different industries. Without the need for bulky equipment for seizure monitoring, you could capture real-life data for diagnoses. Fitness tattoos that monitor signs, blood pressure, and heart rate throughout your day-to-day activities could be made and connected to your smart phone. Cranes could be directed by very precise hand gestures by someone on the ground close to the action.

Why did I choose the Rogers Group? Was there something special about John Rogers's team and the work they do? No. I chose him at random. I have a methodology for listening to signals from a wide variety of sources. As I sat down to write this chunk, I looked through my notes and selected him because his website was cool and intrigued me.

A brief inspection of his site reveals that he has dozens of technologies that are in various stages of development. Some are in the imagined future (pre-prototype) and some in the possible future (post-prototype). The leader, John A. Rogers, is wide open for working with entrepreneurs.

Rogers' research includes fundamental and applied aspects of nano and molecular-scale fabrication as well as materials and patterning techniques for unusual electronic and photonic devices, with an emphasis on bio-integrated and bio-inspired systems. He has published more than 350 papers, and is an inventor on over eighty patents and patent applications, more than fifty of which are licensed or in active use by large companies and startups that he has co-founded[33].

The point is that there are thousands of groups like the Rogers Group. Many universities possess groups like this one in different domains. We don't lack for signals of disruptive technologies. We are entering an age of an exponential explosion of new technologies and capabilities. What we lack are entrepreneurs willing to work with them, taking their ideas to market.

> **Key Thought: We don't lack for signals of disruptive technologies. We lack the Entrepreneurs willing to take them to market.**

Conclusions for the Disruptive Leader

1. The opportunities to create barriers to entry are greater now than they have ever been. Universities and governments support inventors developing new capabilities across multiple exponential technologies.
2. With the Internet, these inventors and their prototypes are easy to find. Search costs are now trivial compared to the days before the Internet.
3. Until you choose to engage in invention, or in bringing an invention to market, your business will always be subject to commoditization.
4. As a disruptive leader, recalibrate management processes to seek out and find technologies in the prototyping stage, or earlier, and bring them into your strategic development process.

Exercise: Take stock of your offerings

1. On what technological and methodological platforms are they based?
2. How much IP protection and how many barriers to entry do they provide?
3. Conversely, how difficult would it be for a well-funded competitor to copy them?
4. What management process is in place to uncover the latest and greatest in technological development occurring in labs and universities?

Chapter 5: The Expert's Paradox

> Those who are expert within a domain are least able to disrupt it.

INTRODUCTION

It's good to know that signals represent the potential to create sustainable differentiated growth. However, signals are useless when we can't recognize them for what they represent. Unfortunately for most of us, we suffer from the paradox that the more we succeed, the more blind we become.

THE EXPERT'S PARADOX

On January 9, 2007, Steve Jobs announced the iPhone. In the associated press release, the author described everything the iPhone was capable of doing and how it did it. What's most revealing was the reaction of the industry players at the time.

Jim Balsillie, now the former co-CEO of RIM stated:

> It is doubtful the device will have much of an impact on RIM's overall sales. For one thing, the iPhone will hold little appeal for RIM's core business market and its need for secure information technology systems, which RIM has been providing for years with its corporate BlackBerry email servers.

Not to be outdone, Steve Ballmer of Microsoft was no better.[34] Laughing, he said:

> Ha ha, $500, fully subsidized with a plan, that's the most expensive phone in the world and it doesn't appeal to business customers because it doesn't have a key-board, which makes it not a very good email machine.

We all know how the story unfolded. By the third quarter of 2013:

- Apple, who started with 0% market share, had become the most profitable vendor of smartphones.
- RIM (Research in Motion), previously in second place at 40 per-cent share, was teetering on bankruptcy.
- Nokia, with 55 percent share, had been sold to Microsoft and continued to struggle.

The launch of the iPhone was not some distant signal, never before seen. The iPhone was right in the middle of their domain, and these companies blew it. Why? These are bright people who built and ran multibillion dollar enterprises.

I've worked with people in over forty industries. Recently, in working with a number of commercial construction companies, I came across a signal from China about a company that built a thirty-story hotel in fifteen days.[35] When I say *built*, I don't mean that they built the shell. I mean the built it completely, including installing the furniture.

During a time-lapse video of the build, the narrator mentions that the building:

1. Can resist a magnitude 9.0 earthquake and is five times more resistant than traditional buildings.
2. Is five times more energy efficient than comparable buildings.
3. Has twenty times purer air.

Now, everyone I've told this story to outside of the construction industry had a "Say goodnight to construction as we know it" moment. However, everyone inside the industry gave me a litany of reasons why it wouldn't work: regulations, architectural issues, union concerns, engineering problems, and contractor resistance. Their reasons were complete with stories about how they had tried to change things in the past and it never worked. To make matters worse, this signal comes from the knowable future. The Broad Company in China didn't make a prototype of how they *might* build a thirty-story hotel in fifteen days. They *built* the hotel in fifteen days.

This reaction is the same for most people with whom I've worked in industries such as beverage distribution, education, and publishing. Why is this true? Why are people in an industry so blind to what is obvious to those outside it?

Some people suggest it is arrogance or hubris. I don't buy that. I've worked with too many entrepreneurs to think that they are anything other than the most dedicated, hardworking, straightforward, tell-it-like-it-is people I've ever had the pleasure to work with. No, it's not arrogance. I've learned that two other factors are at play:

personal expertise and technical language. This chapter deals with the first factor.

HOW PERSONAL EXPERTISE BLINDS US

Sport coaches talk about *muscle memory*, the phenomenon whereby an athlete practices so much that the reaction to a given situation become instinctive. Malcolm Gladwell,[36] in his books *Blink* and *Outliers*, describes how this phenomenon includes all experts in their given domains. He writes that the magic number is ten thousand hours. After ten thousand hours of practice in any domain (athletics, music, ancient art, business, or physics), an expert instinctively knows what works and doesn't work.

His hypothesis has been validated by research into how the neocortex in the brain functions. The neocortex, the part of the brain in which we hold conscious thought, acts as a giant parallel processor. As we think, we do not process the inputs as a computer does, one bit at a time. Rather, we process in parallel, in the search for recognizable patterns. It turns out that experts (medical experts, chess masters, hockey players) have mastered about one hundred thousand patterns. When they think about an issue or opportunity, their brains (and hence our brains) are processing all these patterns simultaneously to find the one with the best fit.

Consequently, when we reach this expert stage, the neurons in our brains are hardwired to find the right answer to a new situation in the blink of an eye. Our perspective on what works and doesn't work makes us extremely efficient. Like muscle memory, our personal expertise becomes a great asset. The more we succeed, the more our personal expertise gets reinforced until it becomes an unconscious skill. It becomes a gift of knowing with certainty whether something will work or not. Because our expertise was built up over such a large experience base, 99.5 percent of the time these instinctive responses are correct.

After we make a lightning fast decision and someone asks how we knew that it would work, we justify it by finding reasons. But that's not how we arrived at the decision. We arrived at that decision instinctively, in an instant. Only when asked do we find reasons why it's true. That's how Wayne Gretzky knew to pass the puck to where the player would be. He didn't decide. He knew instinctively. All experts behave this way.

> **Key thought: like muscle memory, our personal expertise makes us extremely efficient when dealing *inside* our area of expertise.**

So in one sense, Jim Balsillie and Steve Balmer were correct. At the time of the iPhone announcement, RIM knew exactly what the smartphone market wanted. After all, they had created it. You just need to look at the history of RIM to see it. RIM didn't appear overnight. They started in 1998 by turning the Ericsson-developed Mobitex wireless data network into a wireless e-mail network. It ultimately led to the launch of the BlackBerry in 2002. Along the way, its market (large enterprises who could afford the phone) provided strong feedback to them about what they wanted from BlackBerry: security and push services. That learning led their growth from $294,000 in 2002 to $3 billion in 2007.

With more than ten thousand hours of experience in the marketplace, Jim Balsillie and Steve Ballmer both evaluated the iPhone against what was, not what could be. The brain looks for preexisting fit patterns and the neocortexes of these two executives couldn't find one. There was nothing in their brains that matched what the iPhone was about. In fact, the opposite was true. The pattern of the iPhone was missing key ingredients that they knew with certainty were required to be successful. They knew with the certainty that comes from listening to a market that took RIM from less than $1 million to $3 billion in five years.

That's bad enough, except it's made worse by the amygdala. Those two little almond-shaped glands sit deep within the brain and control our fight-or-flight response. From an evolutionary standpoint, we exist today as a species because our ancestors instinctively knew whether to fight or run. Our ancestors couldn't take time to debate whether the shape in the shadows was a lion or not. They needed to act! Consequently, we never evolved the biological systems to evaluate opportunities. So when we are confronted with anything new, we only evaluate its risk potential.[37]

> **Key Thought: In new situations, humans are sensitive to risk. Conversely, we are desensitized to opportunity.**

When confronted with a pattern that does not fit, the neocortex sends a signal to the amygdala, which processes it to determine the appropriate fight-or-flight response. All this happens in an instant. Either way, the amygdala only provides a negative response. What happens next is standardized. Various hormones and adrenaline are released in line with the level of threat so as to increase heart rate, blood pressure, and respiration. The result is that experts not only know intellectually that the idea they are listening to is wrong, they physically and emotionally *feel* it as well. That is why their rejections can be so fierce.

> **Key thought: In a world of increasing disruption, our biology fails us. The amygdala doesn't do engage.**

The patterns that experts build up over time are only valid as long as their environment stays the same. When the environment changes,[38] or when a signal arrives that portends such a change, their one hundred thousand patterns now work against them. Those well-connected neurons inside their neocortex that made them so wise turn out to act as their own personal antibodies to the potential game-changer in front of them.

> **Key thought: Our expertise becomes a personal antibody when working outside our domain expertise.**

Of course, we are all experts[39] in our own way. Combine our instinctive risk-sensitive reaction with a deep understanding of "our" norm and we get a toxic response. Our minds are flooded with a tidal wave of risk perception. The more experience we have, the more risks we can see. The bigger and more disruptive the idea, the taller the incoming tsunami of rejection we experience.

This chain of events is what creates the "it won't work here" response of experts. It's not stupidity. It's not arrogance. It's human biology and the gift of expertise that creates what I call the *expert's paradox*. When disrupting, our greatest strength becomes our greatest weakness.

Our greatest strength (our vast experience) fails us when it comes to situations that fall outside our norm. Tragically, that's what signals portend. They are the signs from the future about to arrive concerning the disruption of the present norm. That's the expert's paradox. Our greatest strength becomes our greatest weakness[40] when we attempt to think and imagine a disruptive world (a new offering, business model, or industry norm).

In the face of their deep feelings of overwhelming risk, it's extremely hard for the expert to imagine a new disruptive reality. Hence, the people best able to work in a norm are the least able to imagine its disruption. Their expertise creates personal antibodies.

Finally, because experts are typically older and have proven themselves, they often find themselves in positions of power. This leads to a common complaint in many organizations that leadership won't listen to the young and their bold, market-disrupting ideas.

> **The people best able to lead in a norm are the least able to imagine its disruption.**

The stories above are not unique. The majority of enterprises and industries are not disrupted by insiders, but by outsiders who have not built up the same personal expertise. The outsiders don't "know" any better and so they don't have the antibodies that tell them what won't work.

Is there no hope for those of us who have reached mastery? Does the expert's paradox keep us from playing a significant role in inventing and bringing to market a disruptor? Are we forever trapped in our personal expert's paradox with no way out?

Yes, there is hope. Yes, there is a highly significant role we can play as experts that utilizes our expertise. And no, we are not forever trapped in the expert's paradox.

Dealing with the Expert's Paradox

Like those who attend Alcoholics Anonymous, we first have to admit we have a problem.

The following exercise helps us identify our own personal expertise and its impact on our ability to see and adapt signals to create those big, bold ideas. A PDF version of this exercise can be downloaded at www.johnsutherlandbooks.com.

> **Tip: engage your team in this exercise so all members can recognize when personal antibodies are at play.**

THE PERSONAL ANTIBODY EXERCISE

Complete the following form.

Figure 10. Expert's Paradox

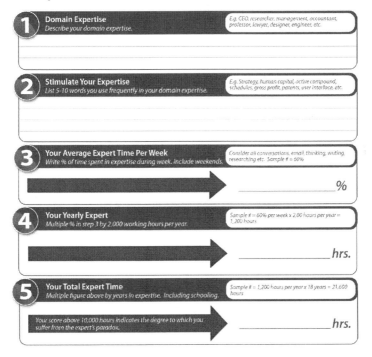

Examples of Calculated Domain Expertise:

2000 working hrs × 50% of usage = 1000 hours × 10 years = 10,000 hours

2000 working hrs × 60% of usage = 1200 hours × 12 years = 14,400 hours

2000 working hrs × 70% of usage = 1400 hours × 15 years = 21,000 hours

2000 working hrs × 80% of usage = 1600 hours × 7 years = 11,200 hours

2000 working hrs × 90% of usage = 1800 hours × 20 years = 36,000 hours

That number represents our personal expertise and perspective on life. We filter ideas first through our personal perspective. It is our dominant view of life.

Now, compare your number to ten thousand hours. That's the measure of the strength of your personal expertise. It's why you succeed. It's why you instinctively, and ninety-nine times out of one hundred, correctly know whether something will work or fail. We've all heard the expression "think outside the box." It's not that we can't think outside the box. The issue is we *are* the box and our number represents the thickness of its walls.

Feel Your Antibodies

Now that you've calculated the depth of your expertise (and your antibodies), read the following excerpts from Ray Kurweil's recent book

How to Create a Mind in which he predicts we will be transferring our brains to computers by some time in the 2040s.[41]

> In a talk at the 2009 TED conference at Oxford, Markram said, "It is not impossible to build a human brain, and we can do it in ten years." His most recent target for a full-brain simulation is 2023.

So while it could be simulated, how would your brain be uploaded? The excerpt continues:

> I would not expect such an "uploading" technology to be available until around the 2040s. (The computational requirements to simulate a brain at that degree of precision, which I estimate to be 10^{19} calculations per second, will be available in supercomputers according to my projections by the early 2020s; however, the necessary nondestructive brain scanning technologies will take longer.)

Do you feel disbelief, dismissive? Or, did you find yourself thinking that you couldn't wait for it to happen? Of course you didn't. The idea that we will transfer our brains into a computer is ludicrous. There is nothing in any one of our experiences that would allow us to make a good fit to that pattern of thoughts. Next he'll suggest we can fly to the moon.

The Good News

We can't undo our personal expertise (our box), nor should we. After all, it is our greatest strength. But what we can do is learn to recognize when our box is acting as a personal antibody and then grow it to appropriately inspect game-changing, disruptive ideas.

To do that, we need to learn how to recognize and deal with personal perspectives that turn into antibodies.

How to Recognize When Expertise Turns into Antibodies

Recognizing when antibodies occur is all about the speed at which we react in new situations. You will feel antibodies under the following conditions:

1. The presentation, conversation, or dialogue deals with ideas and proposals that fall outside the norm of how business is conducted. It sounds and feels different and radical.
2. As the conversation progresses, your mind quickly and instinctively brings up multiple objections. "This won't work, distributors will reject this, there are no customers for this, and the regulations won't allow it."
3. Emotionally, you attach negative feelings to the idea being discussed. Thoughts of how stupid something is and the aspects that haven't been considered quickly come to mind.
4. You feel flushed and your heart beats faster.

Dealing with Antibodies

In situations in which you are considering ideas or proposals outside the norm and your feelings are similar to those above, do the following:

1. If you are presenting, warn your audience at the outset that the idea is outside the norm. This tactic will socialize the audience to be conscious of their expertise turning into antibodies.
2. If you are a recipient of the idea and find yourself quickly dismissing the idea, explicitly state that your "antibodies are screaming at you."[42] This tactic will alert the presenter that they need to slow down and make sure you have the data you need.

3. If you declare antibodies are at work, visually imagine taking your expertise box, stepping outside it, and stepping into a disruptor box.

> **Key Thought: Making our personal antibodies explicitly known socializes everyone to help each other consider the possibilities inherent in disruptors.**

Conclusions for the Disruptive Leader

1. The single biggest barrier to becoming a disruptive leader is you and your expertise.
2. Run the exercise for key people in the organization so everyone recognizes their own internal antibodies.
3. As a disruptive leader, recalibrate how you view barriers and think of them as uncertainties that represent potential opportunities. This will help you develop sustainable IP protection.

Exercise: Test Your Internal Antibodies

Note: this exercise has the greatest payoff of any exercise in this book.

1. Read Ray Kurzweil's book *The Singularity is Here* or some other outlandish reading.
2. Stop when you're reading to feel the sensations your body produces: incredulity, tension.
3. Say to your conscious mind that it is just a signal from the imaginary future.
4. To move your mind from focusing on the barriers to considering who might invent a new method or technology to overcome that barrier.

5. Remind yourself that it took 104 years to get to the moon after Jules Verne published his book. What people thought about that book is what people now think about Ray's book.
6. Now inspect your feelings again to assess the strength of your personal antibodies.

Chapter 6: The Universal Value Canvas

The previous chapter dealt with the personal expertise barrier to becoming a disruptive leader. This chapter deals with the second barrier: technical language.

LANGUAGE AS A BARRIER

It's not English or German or Chinese or any other language that is a barrier. I'm referring to the language of *ideas*. Mathematics has its own language. So too do physics, biology, finance, and marketing. They all have terms with definitions that mean something specific and unique to them. $E=mc^2$ has a specific meaning that transcends time and space. It doesn't matter what century it is, what business you operate, or who you are. $E=mc^2$ is a universal truth that applies in all circumstances across all time. It's independent of circumstance. That's equally true for ROI in finance or DNA structures in biology. These are examples of technical languages that can be shared no matter what tongue you speak.

What is important about a technical language is its degree of universality. Take calculus, for example. The problem of calculating volume existed for thousands of years. How much beer does that barrel contain and therefore how much should I pay for it? In the time of Sir Isaac

Newton, the methods to calculate volume were long and laborious (such as breaking the barrel into smaller and smaller parts, calculating the volume in the pieces and adding them together). Calculus, with its new terms and formulas, changed all that. Volume could be calculated in a matter of minutes. More importantly, it didn't matter what kind of volume you needed to calculate, whether it was on Earth or somewhere else in the universe. The formulas worked everywhere.

Life is like that. There are universal truths about how things work. It doesn't matter whether the wing is from an eagle or a 747, the calculations for lift are the same. It's not just the hard sciences like mathematics or physics that have universal truths either, although they excel at producing them. It applies to other human interests as well: biology, genetics, materials, and finance.

Some of these fields employ formulas. Others do not. That doesn't matter. What they hold in common is that each has discovered a pattern that applies universally across time, space, and circumstance. Embedded in that pattern are terms with definitions that describe the pattern and how we, as humans, relate to it.

What about the creation of value? What are the universal truths about this human endeavor that hold true for commercial enterprises, artists, and philosophers alike? How many universal truths can we name (with terms and definitions) that explain how value is created across all times and in all environments?

Most of us can't. That's why we can't see. It's not about intelligence or skills. We lack a universal frame of reference. We lack an understanding of the universal pattern of value creation that would be as true today as it was two hundred years ago, two thousand years ago, or two hundred thousand years ago.

In the absence of these universal truths, we are left with explaining value creation from our own perspective, with our own terms and definitions. We have no choice but to filter everything through our personal experience and expertise. For RIM, Nokia, and Microsoft, that experience was about secure information technology systems and e-mails. For a beverage bottler, it's about cases sold. For Sony, it was about the volume of albums sold through distribution channels. For hospitals, it's about patient throughput. For car manufactures, it's about performance and brand positioning. What is it about for you? Think about your own industry terms.

By utilizing the universal pattern of value creation described in this chapter, we step outside our industry language to discuss ideas and projects in a universal language centered on the disruption of human behavior spaces. Working in this common language, along with recognizing when personal antibodies are at play, tempers the inevitable risk sensations that flare up when we butt up against our expertise.

But what is value? What does the dictionary definition of value tell us about the creation of value during usage? *Value* is defined as the "worth of something in terms of the amount of other things for which it can be exchanged or in terms of some medium of exchange."[43]

The dictionary defines value during the acquisition stage of an offering. It tells us nothing about the value we receive during its usage. Nor does it tell us anything about how that value is created.

To build successful disruptors, we need to be able to generate alternative scenarios that we can compare based on the level of value they can create. The Value Designer Canvas does exactly that. It provides a common language platform to both create strategic disruptor scenarios and compare them across diverse situations for their value-creation capacity.

This canvas platform is not the first of its kind. Alex Osterwalder's Business Model Canvas[44] provided "a shared understanding and common language" for discussing a business model. The hidden genius behind his canvas concept was his discovery of the limited number of concepts and associated questions required to describe *any* business model. While there are millions of questions we could ask about a business model, Alex organized and limited them to the critical few.

That discovery and the canvas structure that flowed from it allowed users to compare any business model to any other, and in so doing, transfer success in one industry or situation to another.

The Value Designer Canvas follows the same principles.

> **Key Thought: There are a limited number of concepts and associated questions that need be applied to successfully design a disruptive offering for any situation.**

VALUE DESIGNER CANVAS

We know how value is assessed during acquisition. But how is value created? I define *value creation* as "the expansion of relationship space from changed behavioral norms enabled by a disruptor."

Figure 11. Value Designer Canvas

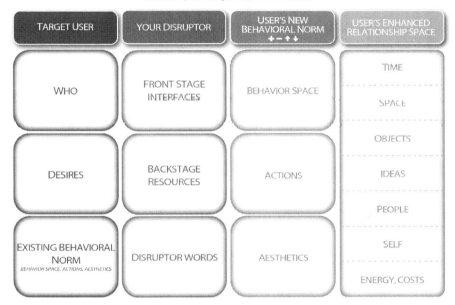

The Value Designer Canvas
16 factors capture the dynamics of value creation

TARGET USER	YOUR DISRUPTOR	USER'S NEW BEHAVIORAL NORM	USER'S ENHANCED RELATIONSHIP SPACE
WHO	FRONT STAGE INTERFACES	BEHAVIOR SPACE	TIME
			SPACE
			OBJECTS
DESIRES	BACKSTAGE RESOURCES	ACTIONS	IDEAS
			PEOPLE
EXISTING BEHAVIORAL NORM *BEHAVIOR SPACE, ACTIONS, AESTHETICS*	DISRUPTOR WORDS	AESTHETICS	SELF
			ENERGY, COSTS

Overall Structure

As the canvas illustrates, four elements describe how value is created. Inside these four elements reside the sixteen factors that interact with each other during value creation.

The four elements are:

1) The target user
2) Your disruptor
3) The user's new behavioral norm
4) The user's enhanced relationship space (benefits received)

Figure 12. The universal pattern of value creation

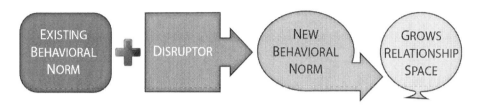

Target users live their lives in an existing behavioral norm. They add an offering (a disruptor) to their lives and interact with it. In interacting with the offering, the target creates a new behavioral norm, from which benefits flow in the form of enhancements to their relationships. The degree of satisfaction with the benefits received determines the targets' stickiness with the offering.

Note: To learn the canvas, we start at the end – 4 – and work back to 1.

Element 4: User's Enhanced Relationship Space

Figure 13. Value Canvas: Enhanced Relationship Space

An offering, in its usage, creates value by improving the goodness in users' lives. But what is the measure of that improvement? All lives are different. What do we hold in common that allows us to assess improvement in our lives across all situations, across all time? What we all hold in common is our relationships. There are seven types of relationships that define our lives. At any moment of our lives, all of these relationships are at play. Collectively, how we interact with them in the moment determines our happiness, the goodness we feel in our lives. When any combination of them improves, so too the quality of our lives improve.

We benefit from interacting with an offering when our relationships improve.

Relationship: A connection, association, or involvement.

Relationship Space: For any individual, the sum of all positive and negative relationships across seven dimensions.

The Seven Relationships Factors

1) Time: When we are
2) Space: Where we are
3) Self: Who we are, and who we want to be
4) People: By themselves and in groups
5) Objects: Inanimate and living
6) Ideas: How and why we are
7) Energy: The power and costs we consume

Example: You are sitting in a car waiting to go to a meeting that will not start for another forty-five minutes. It's a warm, late spring day and your co-worker is sitting beside you discussing the day you've spent together. The windows are open and a warm breeze wafts over you. Everything that you experience in the next forty-five minutes is describable from a relationship perspective. She and you:

1) Are situated in *time*. It's a forty-five-minute period on June 11, 2013. You feel somewhat irked that you have this time to kill but that is more than compensated for by the quality of the conversation.

2) Are situated in *space*. You are parked on Penn Avenue in Pittsburgh. The air is warm, feels pleasant, and so few cars go by that any exhaust fumes do not trouble you. You hear the trees rustling and there is a hint of flowers in the air. All quite pleasant.

3) Engage with yourself (*self*). You think and evaluate what she is saying. She does the same. Your minds actively find patterns to answer each other's questions.

4) Engage with each other (*people*). You communicate your thoughts. You strengthen your relationship. She does likewise.

5) Interact with *objects* (animate and inanimate). You sit on a seat in a car. It's comfortable. You touch the window controls to move them up and down.

6) Express and hold *ideas*. You discuss a range of concepts. Much of what you express about the day's events are grounded in the concepts (principles, values) that you hold dear.

7) Finally, you expend *energy*. Your body converts energy stores into the actions of speaking, sitting, and holding yourself upright in the seat. Later, you move to a small pub across the street, where you buy a beer. You pay for it with money,[45] a form of stored energy.

> **Key thought: We receive value from an offering when it improves our seven relationships: time, space, self, people, objects, ideas, and energy.**

Collectively, our seven relationships constitute our *relationship space*. Our relationship space acts like a balloon. The positive relationships blow air into our relationship space balloon. The negative relationships act as holes in our relationship balloon, shrinking its overall size. If we could add up all our relationships, taking into account the good and the bad, we could conceptually measure the size and quality of our lives. We could compute for ourselves the size of our relationship space balloon. We feel value when our relationship space expands.

> **Key thought: We are born alone with nothing but our seven relationships. How we manage our relationships determines the quality and goodness of our lives.**

Element #3 New Behavioral Norm

Figure 14. Value Canvas: A User's New Behavioral Norm

But how does our relationship space expand? What mechanism creates the change in our lives that improves our relationship space? We live in our own personal world of behaviors: the things we do to achieve the goals we set out for ourselves. Changing our behaviors impacts our relationships, for good or bad. As creatures of habit we, by definition, have favored behaviors. Changing these behaviors by adding, subtracting, enhancing, or reducing them changes our relationships.

New behavioral norm: The regular or habitual behavior spaces exhibited by an individual or group in the expression of their desires.

Three factors describe a user's behavioral norm:

- Behavior space
- Actions
- Aesthetics

How and why does relationship space expand when a user interacts with an offering? It expands because, in interacting with the offering, a new behavioral norm emerges.

New behavioral norms emerge because of four types of changes that disruptors have on the three factors (behavior space, actions, and aesthetics). For each behavior space, action, or aesthetic, the disruptor can:

1) Enhance a factor
2) Reduce a factor
3) Add a factor
4) Eliminate a factor

These are the same types of changes first identified by Renée Mauborgne and Chan Kim in *Blue Ocean Strategy*.[46] They utilized them to compare performance dimensions between competing offerings. They are utilized here in mapping direct changes in users' behavioral norms. Changes in performance dimensions may or may not impact users. For example, an increase in the sophistication of Microsoft Word will not affect users who only use it to create simple documents.

Factor 1: Behavior Space

Behavior: An observable activity in a human (in the expression of a desire).

Example: Making a call from a smartphone to wish a friend happy birthday.

Behavior Space: The sum of all behaviors deployed by users in the expression of their desires and goals.

Behavior space is analogous to Clayton Christensen's "job to be done."[47] We live in a rich behavioral world. For example, there exist a wide variety of behaviors available when wishing to communicate happy birthday. If we added up all the behaviors available to wish someone happy birthday, we would have defined the behavioral universe for that desire. But people use only a limited subset of all the available behaviors. This subset defines that person's behavior space for wishing someone happy birthday. Equally, there are behavior spaces for other desires: communicating, creating, traveling, and eating. As such, behavior spaces are related to the context in which the person finds him- or herself.

As creatures of habit, we typically work with only a limited subset of behaviors available. Over time, we develop habits and those behavior spaces become normative. We have our favorites with which we have grown comfortable. Changing them is hard to do. To be successful, offerings need to disrupt the behavioral norm. That's why the canvas labels offerings as *disruptors*, to reinforce their key purpose.

As an example, the advent of mobile phones allowed users to:

- Add communicating by phone from any location.
- Reduce or eliminate making phone calls from pay phones.
- Grow the number of calls made.

> **Key thought: The behavioral universe is gigantic. As creatures of habit, our personal behavior space is limited to the favored few. Offerings need to work hard to disrupt that norm.**

Factor 2: Actions

Actions: The steps taken by a user to use an offering.

In a perfect world, when I want to talk to my friend to wish her happy birthday, I'd think about that and our minds would connect automatically. There would be no time or energy expenditure required. We would think it and it would happen. We don't live in that world...yet.[48] Today, we have to take a series of actions to make that connection. These steps are always a waste of time and energy, but are necessary to achieve our behavioral goal. Reducing the number of steps and actions required or increasing the simplicity and intuitiveness of these actions always makes a winning offering.

Think about all the steps required to launch the phone app on an iPhone.

1. Press home button.
2. Swipe to open.

3. Press contact button.
4. Scroll to find contact.
5. Press contact.
6. Press number.

All the above actions are a waste of time and energy. They provide no inherent value. The value comes only from the behavior of making the phone call. All the steps taken to enable that behavior are useless and become the basis to further improve and differentiate your offering.

> **Key thought: All actions required to enable the behavior are superfluous. Eliminating actions is *always* a winning strategy.**

Factor 3: Aesthetics

Aesthetics: The beauty, pleasures, and hazards to which one is exposed when using a disruptor.

Offerings differ in their aesthetic impact during use. As users, we are not only attracted by the functionality an offering provides, but by its sensual stimulation as well. Its touch, beauty, smell, taste, and sound combine together to stimulate our interest and emotional well-being. As a species, we are driven by our pleasure centers. Objects, processes, and ideas that appeal to our sense of beauty stimulate those centers. In the battle to differentiate, stimulating our senses creates desire. This is why Disneyworld parks pump the exhaust from the bakery into Main Street.

Examples of the aesthetic are the smoothness of a fabric, or conversely, the dust created when opening a bag of cement.

> **Key Thought: Designing an offering that pleasures the five senses and removes hazards (negative aesthetics) is always a winning strategy.**

Element 2: Your Disruptor

Figure 15. Value Canvas: Your Disruptor

The disruptor acts as the active agent in the creation of value. This element is the only element that is controlled by the organization. All other elements describe the user.

Factor 1: Front-stage Interfaces

Front-stage interfaces: The objects, ideas, processes, or combinations thereof with which the target interacts.

There is a direct link between the design, form, and functionality of all the interfaces that make up the disruptor and its ability to disrupt an existing behavioral norm and replace it with a new norm. The next flavor of Oreo cookie will have a negligible impact[49] on behavioral norms by comparison to a universal translation app on your smartphone. The design of the interface should address each of the three behavioral norm factors: behavior space, actions, and aesthetics.

Design your interface to:

1. *Enable new behaviors and capabilities to emerge.* Think how mobile phones allowed people to "make phone calls from anywhere," a new behavior. Or, think about how FedEx enabled the delivery of packages overnight, a new behavior. What will be the new behaviors your offering enables in the pursuit human desires?
2. *Eliminate actions.* As stated above, all actions needed to enable a behavior are wasteful. Design your interface so it eliminates as many actions as possible. That is why voice activation is becoming more prevalent. It eliminates the action we call typing.
3. *Stimulate the senses.* Eliminate hazards and make usage pleasurable. When our senses are pleased, we engage fully.

Example: The following are examples of front-stage interfaces:

- Objects: iPhone, cars, hamburgers.
- Ideas: calculus formulas, ROI analysis, goal setting, nonviolent revolution.
- Processes: serving line at a buffet, registering a car, sending a FedEx package.

Factor 2: Back-stage Resources

Back-stage resources: The required assets, capabilities, and partnerships that make the front-stage interfaces functional.

Interfaces often do not work by themselves. They are dependent upon resources hidden to the user.

Examples: All electric devices depend upon electrical generation. Smartphones are dependent upon cellular carrier networks and the Internet.

Factor 3: Disruptor Words

Disruptor Words: The new terms or labels created to describe the offering or the new behavior.

Hanging a label on the disruptor makes communicating the new offering easy to understand.

Example: Interface label: Twitter and tweets. New behavior label: tweeting.

Element 1: Target User

Figure 16. Value Canvas: Target User

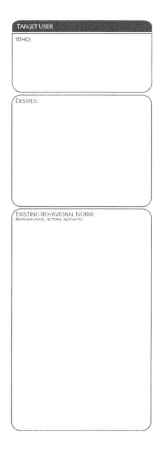

Finally, to disrupt we need to know our target users for disruption and understand their context.

Three factors capture target users and their context:

1) Who
2) Desires
3) Existing behavioral norm

Factor 1: Who

Who: The target individuals or groups that use the offering.

Users come in many types: users of the offering, purchasers, technical buyers, influencers, and specifiers. Understanding the context of each user type is necessary to create a complete understanding of the behavioral norm that you are trying to disrupt.

Example: Disrupting the commercial construction business in the laying of cement floors entails understanding the following users: the owner, architect, engineer, general contractor, unions, municipalities, cement contractor, and flooring contractor. Each one plays a role. Expanding the *who* to include all roles played creates the chance to see hidden disruption opportunities.

Factor 2: Desires

Desires: The wants, cravings and wishes the offering is intended to address.

Desires are independent of the proposed offering and are categorized by Maslow's hierarchy of needs. Desires vary by user and their role in the offering's use life cycle.

Example: People don't want a three-quarter inch drill bit, which is an offering. They want a three-quarter inch hole, an outcome. How can you create deliver three-quarter inch holes without using a drill bit? 3-D printing.

Factor 3: Existing Behavioral Norm

Existing Behavioral Norm: The behavior spaces, actions, and aesthetics currently demonstrated by the target in the expression of their desires and goals. These three factors were defined in *New Behavioral Norm* (Element 3).

To disrupt a behavioral norm, first map the existing one. Look for joys and pains in the three areas: behavior space, actions, and aesthetics.

THE UNIVERSAL VALUE-DESIGNER SUMMARY

Successful offerings, be they objects, ideas, or processes (commercial or not), all follow a common usage pattern that defines why they provide value to the user, and so are adopted. Design your offering with the universal pattern in mind and your chance of adoption by users will increase. *Value creation* is defined as the expansion of relationship space from changed behavioral norms enabled by a disruptor. Summarized below are the principles of this pattern.

Principles

1) As humans, we share common traits, one of which is our desires.
2) Our lives are made up of a collection of seven relationships: time and space, people and self, ideas and objects, and energy. Our lives are our relationships. To improve people's lives, improve these relationships.
3) We all seek more goodness in our lives. Consequently, it is the improvements in our relationships that define the satisfaction we feel with our lives. Offerings that improve our relationships are valued. Value is the perceived improvement in our relationships.
4) The net satisfaction with all our relationships defines our relationship space. It's analogous to a balloon. When one or more of our relationships improves (expands), we feel satisfied. When one or more relationships contract, we feel bad. The impact of

"something" on our relationships is how we assess the goodness or badness of it.

5) As creatures of habit, we embrace and engage with our favorite things, be they objects, ideas, or processes.

6) Using these things allows for the behaviors that enable us to achieve the goals driven by our desires.

    a. The thing we call a *phone* enables the behavior we call *the phone call.*

    b. The phone call enables us to achieve the desire of communicating with someone.

    c. We feel satisfied because the reduction in effort of the phone call (compared to walking to talk to the person) improves our time and energy relationship.

    d. When we feel satisfied on multiple occasions, over time, we adopt the new thing, *the phone* and its behavior – *phone calls* – into our behavioral norm.

7) This favored collection of things and the behaviors they facilitate define our behavior space.

8) Behavior space is comprised of three factors: the behavior itself, the actions, and the aesthetics.

    a. The behavior is the phone call

    b. The actions are the steps required to connect to the correct number and dial it.

    c. The aesthetics are the smoothness of the device, the clarity of sound, and its form.

9) Our habitual use of our favored things establishes our personal behavioral norm.

10) Our relationships change when our behaviors change. The larger the change in behaviors, the larger the impact on our relationships.

    a. Disasters are devastating because of the severe constriction they impose on our behaviors. Remove electricity, readily available drinking water, and shelter from the environment and the behaviors available to achieve our desires are likewise restricted. In the absence of those behaviors, our relationships shrink dramatically.

b. Conversely, offerings are successful because they improve our relationships.

11) New offerings and disasters are both disruptive phenomena (one good, one bad). They act by disrupting our behavioral norms, and in so doing, expand or contract our relationship space.

12) New offerings (objects, ideas, and processes) disrupt behavioral space by adding, subtracting, enhancing, or reducing each of the three factors listed in number 8, above. The larger the disruption of behavioral norms, the larger the impact on relationships.

13) Therefore, when designing an offering, to transform it into a disruptor, focus its design exclusively on the impact it has on human behavioral norms:

a. the behavior space changes
b. the action changes
c. the aesthetic changes

14) The value the new offering creates for the intended user relates directly to the degree to which those design elements significantly change the behavioral norm and its impact on relationship space.

Figure 17. Business Model Generation Mapped On The Value Designer Canvas

As Alex Osterwalder was first to originate the canvas methodology, I've chosen to illustrate his *Business Model Generation* book and canvas.

The Value Designer Canvas

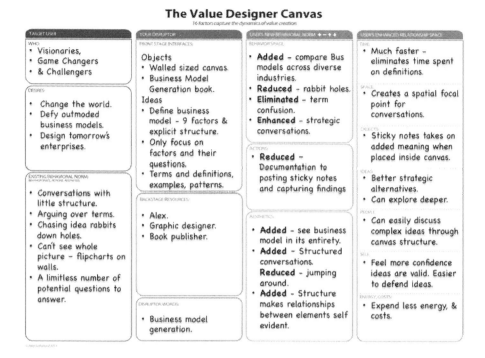

16 factors capture the dynamics of value creation

TARGET USER

WHO:
* Visionaries,
* Game Changers
* & Challengers

DESIRES:
* Change the world.
* Defy outmoded business models.
* Design tomorrow's enterprises.

EXISTING BEHAVIORAL NORM:
* Conversations with little structure.
* Arguing over terms.
* Chasing idea rabbits down holes.
* Can't see whole picture – flipcharts on walls.
* A limitless number of potential questions to answer.

YOUR DISRUPTOR

FRONT STAGE INTERFACES:

Objects
* Walled sized canvas.
* Business Model Generation book.

Ideas
* Define business model – 9 factors & explicit structure.
* Only focus on factors and their questions.
* Terms and definitions, examples, patterns.

BACKSTAGE RESOURCES:
* Alex.
* Graphic designer.
* Book publisher.

DISRUPTOR WORDS:
* Business model generation.

USER'S NEW BEHAVIORAL NORM ◆ ← ↑ ↓

BEHAVIOR SPACE:
* **Added** – compare Bus models across diverse industries.
* **Reduced** – rabbit holes.
* **Eliminated** – term confusion.
* **Enhanced** – strategic conversations.

ACTIONS:
* **Reduced** – Documentation to posting sticky notes and capturing findings.

AESTHETICS:
* **Added** – see business model in its entirety.
* **Added** – Structured conversations. **Reduced** – jumping around.
* **Added** – Structure makes relationships between elements self evident.

USER'S ENHANCED RELATIONSHIP SPACE

TIME:
* Much faster – eliminates time spent on definitions.

SPACE:
* Creates a spatial focal point for conversations.

OBJECTS:
* Sticky notes takes on added meaning when placed inside canvas.

IDEAS:
* Better strategic alternatives.
* Can explore deeper.

PEOPLE:
* Can easily discuss complex ideas through canvas structure.

SELF:
* Feel more confidence ideas are valid. Easier to defend ideas.

ENERGY, COSTS:
* Expend less energy, & costs.

Note: The Value Designer Canvas completed for Alex's Business Model theory was based on the launch of his book. It does not include new disruptive effects from the app, website, or other additions.

Conclusions for the Disruptive Leader

1. The organization needs to be intimately familiar with how their users use their offerings. Examine users' behavioral norms.
2. The greatest opportunity to differentiate your offering comes by looking at users through a behavioral lens, assessing new offerings' impact on enhancing behavioral change, and improving user relationships.

3. As a disruptive leader, you need to recalibrate the language people use to describe current and proposed offerings. Focus on existing behavioral norms and how the offering, in the form of a disruptor, will disrupt that norm and replace it with an improved behavioral norm.

Exercise: Play with the Value Designer Canvas

1. Map your best offering on the canvas. Compare it to your best competitor's offering. Whose offering:

    o   Provides the widest range of new behaviors and capabilities for users to achieve the goals emanating from their desires?
    o   Has the least number of actions to enable the behavior? Whose is the easiest to use?
    o   Is the most pleasing to use with the least amount of hazards?
    o   Creates the greatest improvements of the users' relationships?

2. How can you change your offering (by focusing on disruptor interfaces) so that it does better in each of the above areas?

Chapter 7: Making Your Future

INTRODUCTION

The Value Designer Canvas is intended to help you have a laser focus on the value created for users. When creating a new offering, we have lots of choices to make about the user experience. The Value Designer Canvas (VDC) lets you play with the design elements of the offering and assess their impact on behavior change. The greater the positive behavior change, the greater the value received by users (because it enables the growth of relationship space). With great relationship growth comes great user stickiness.

In short form, the Value Designer Canvas helps you create awesome value propositions, propositions that make users go crazy for them. So we've reached the point where we can now put some of these pieces together to start answering the question, "How can we make our future?"

To make your future, we need to complete three tasks.

Task One: Use signals to imagine a compelling experience for target users that is not possible today.

As discussed previously, IP is created in the possible and imaginary future. If the idea we imagine for a user experience is completely possible today, we have little chance to protect ourselves. Everything we do is imminently knowable. Others already own whatever IP has been created.

Task Two: Assess our contribution in resolving uncertainty.

Ideas in the imaginary future usually require the collaboration of different entities. As such, IP for each participant is based on the amount of uncertainty-resolution contributed. Our scenario should allow for a significant piece of uncertainty to be resolved by us.

Task Three: Identify a subset of the imagined user experience that we can commercialize now *and* that requires the development of our unique IP contribution.

Imaginary ideas hold too much uncertainty to resolve quickly. Hence they offer the potential for IP protection. We'll need to find a subset of that idea where we can create a compelling enough behavior space growth for target users that they willingly adopt it.

A STORY SET IN THE FUTURE

The first barrier to overcome is imagining a compelling user experience that would seem impossible today. In the future-based story we create, we also need to imagine a portion of it in which we can resolve uncertainties. Until your team can "dream up" such stories, you won't be able to become a disruptive entity. It starts with stories set in the future.

This chapter begins with a story about the future, an imaginary tale of a user and a new offering. The story you are about to read is less than six hundred words long and takes about two minutes to read.

To create this story, I employed the VDC. In this chapter, I'm going to share the story and use it to expose the key elements to focus on.

Embedded in the story are a number of disruptors packaged together to create a new user experience. It describes a disruptive scenario. It's the story of how someone uses a disruptive offering to improve his or her life. What is missing in the story are the uncertainties and how they were resolved, along with the business model elements of how the disruptors were distributed, manufactured, and priced. Nor does it describe in detail any of the organizations that put this disruptor together. That's not important right now. During this first stage, we are primarily concerned with whether we can imagine a disruptive scenario that will attract large number of willing users. After all, if no one is willing to buy our offering, there is no viable business.

Our first test of the willingness of users to buy this offering is whether we get excited about it ourselves. If we don't like our story, then likely no one else will either.

A cautionary note: This story is set in the imaginary future. Depending on your expertise you may feel the expert's paradox. If you do, remind yourself that you can safely ignore your internal antibodies when they flare up. It's just a story, after all.

The Story - Stephanie Takes a Ride

It's 2:00 a.m. as Stephanie steps outside. It's dark, cold, and raining, another November morning. Her children, Gena and Jonathan, are safe in their beds as she opens the car door and says, "Take me to the office." As the car (she calls it Andrew) winds its way through the suburban streets to get on the parkway, she logs on to the company website to check trading in London. Stephanie manages European bond trading for the bank and wants to catch up before trading opens in fifty minutes.

After Andrew drops her off at the office, she tells it, "Follow schedule one," and leaves a message. The car returns home by itself, parks out front, and waits. At 7:45 a.m. her two children walk out, get inside Andrew, and it drives them to school. Before they exit, Andrew tells them that their mother loves them and hopes they do well on today's Math and English exams. They respond, saying, "Thanks, Mom, no worries." Andrew asks if they want to send the message immediately or wait until it drives her home. Saying, "Go ahead, tell her now," they exit the car and catch up to their friends.

Andrew turns on the *available* function and waits for the first fare. Three minutes later, two bids for Andrew's time arrive. Based on a revenue-optimizer algorithm, the car accepts the fare for the longer ride to downtown from a predetermined list of acceptable riders. Downpours are expected later in the morning. The algorithm had taken that into account when deciding that downtown was the best place for a FareCar to be.

Thirty minutes later, the fare is dropped off with the automatic payment deposited from the rider's smartphone. By 2:00 p.m. Andrew is low on gas and pulls into one of the many new full-service gas stations. An attendant fills the car with natural gas and wipes down the back seats. Andrew's system has alerted them that it was time for an oil change, so the attendants do that too. It's all part of the service agreement that automatically monitors Stephaine's car and performs ongoing maintenance without her involvement. One hour later, Andrew is in front of the office as Stephanie exits. The car was forewarned that she was leaving when she confirmed it from her smartphone app. After she gets home, she sends Andrew to the store to pick up the groceries she had purchased earlier that day.

At a dinner dance Saturday night, Stephanie explains to her friends that she doesn't rent her car to make money so much as she didn't like the thought of two and a half tons of metal sitting in a garage downtown all day. By renting her car, fewer people need to buy one. It's her contribution to the environment. She explains that she doesn't worry about people leaving a mess because she only accepts single riders, and the service company has installed devices that inspect for trash after a rider exits. Riders are then tracked by the fare management system and are rated for cleanliness. She explains how she told Andrew to only accept riders with the highest cleanliness ratings. While at the dinner, she releases Andrew to support a local nursing home by driving the residents to the movies.

Unpacking the Story

The story transports us to the future and quickly gives us an understanding of what a disruptive offering might be. A *disruptive scenario*, like this story, is the story of how someone uses a disruptive offering to improve his or her life. At less than six hundred words, it described a future with significant opportunities for companies that participate to differentiate themselves and grow rapidly.

> **Key Thought: The future starts with good disruptive stories.**

The Value Designer Canvas

The story explicitly dealt with two of the VDC elements that join together to make the future:

1) Disruptors (specifically the interfaces, at a high level only).
2) Users' new behavioral norms (at a detailed level).

Stephanie's New Behavioral Norm

Stephanie interacted with a driverless car and various programs and services surrounding it. All those devices, programs, and services combined represent the disruptive offering. What is most important about the story, the critical part above all else, is that in using the car she did not behave in the ways we normally behave today.

The following table compares Stephanie's preexisting behavioral norm to the new behavioral norm resulting from her engagement with the offering.

Table 3. Stephanie's Behavior Space Change

PREVIOUS BEHAVIORAL NORM	NEW BEHAVIORAL NORM **Behavior Space**
• Own car • Drive car to work • Spouse drives children to school • Drive car for gas, service, and all shopping • Park car downtown: pay for space	• Own car (same) • Eliminated driving car to work • Eliminated driving children to school • Eliminated driving car for gas, service • Reduced driving for shopping • Added working in car • Added automatic renting of car • Added automatic sharing of car • Added location-based message delivery: car delivers message when children arrive at school

Actions

• Eliminated parking and costs
• Added voice commands to control car

Aesthetics

• Added monitoring of car for refuse

Prior to this offering, Stephanie had a personal behavior space associated with her car. It was a collection of behaviors unique to her that allowed her to achieve her transportation goals. They are listed in the left-hand column. Some of them she had to accept but did not really want. We park and pay for it because we have no choice.[50]

Now look at the column on the right. If we feel excited or intrigued about the story, it's because we were attracted to and intrigued about the behavior changes. As humans, we instinctively react to stories of behavior change.

Figure 18. Stephanie's Story in the Value Designer Canvas

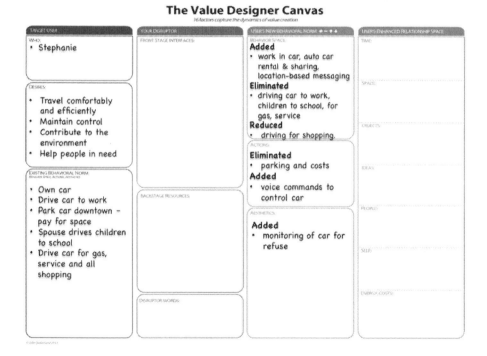

The Disruptors

If you read the story again you'll notice that the disruptors were mostly alluded to, and in some cases were not mentioned at all.

Of course, none of Stephanie's behavior changes could have occurred without her interaction with the disruptors. Below are listed the ten disruptors, in order of appearance, that made this story possible. Most of these disruptors are signals from the future.

1) Driverless cars
2) Voice recognition and commands
3) Programmable car activity schedules ("Run schedule one")
4) Message capture, person recognition, and message relay ("Love you. Good luck.")
5) Rental service that connects renters with car owners
6) Customizable rider selection optimization program ("I only select the cleanest riders.")
7) Automatic payment as part of the fare management system
8) Car operates a status diagnostic with automatic activity generation (buy gas, transmit the need for an oil change)
9) Automated car servicing program
10) Cleanliness-detection devices linked to rider-selection optimization program

Some of these disruptors are here now. A number of companies already give you the ability to rent cars or taxis in some fashion, such as Uber, RelayRides, Getaround, and Enterprise. Some are being prototyped, such as Google's driverless car.[51] Some of them are adaptations of existing services or technologies, such as full service gas stations and optimizing algorithms in other venues. What they have in common is that they all are *signals*. Signs from our future about what we could create.

The Relationship Space Change

Nowhere in the story were Stephanie's relationship space changes explicitly described. All the changes were implied. Why?

When investing in a disruptive offering, we need to communicate it convincingly. A story about how a person using a new offering improves his or her life is the first part of that understanding. We need to visualize it, to experience it. Stories, whether written, role-played, caricatured, or videoed are the most effective way to transfer our imaginary future into the minds of others. We are attracted to stories when they are written in behavioral terms. In reading the story, we can see ourselves in her position and can feel for ourselves how her relationships would improve. As humans, we have sensing systems attuned to a person's behavior. When we read or hear about behavior changes, we instinctively understand what relationship effects they will have, both positive and negative. Leaving it to the mind of the reader makes it more powerful. He or she takes ownership of the relationship impacts.

Table 2 illustrates the relationship changes (value created) Stephanie likely experienced by engaging with the offering and adopting the resultant behavior changes.

Table 4. Stephanie's Changes in Her Relationships

RELATIONSHIP CATEGORY	HOW HER RELATIONSHIPS CHANGED
Time	<ul><li>Turned wasted time in driving to work into productive time.</li><li>Turned wasted time running errands into more enjoyable uses.</li></ul>
Space	<ul><li>Turned inside of car into mini-office.</li></ul>

Objects	• Car becomes a more utilitarian device. Styling will likely become less important in owning a car.
	• The car is no longer limited by needing a driver, so it becomes an asset that can be deployed for other purposes, such as supporting charities.
Ideas	• Having felt the benefits of automation, Stephanie will start to employ that concept in other purchases. She will ask herself, "How does X automate what I need to do so I can save more time?"
People	• Willing to share her car with strangers.
	• She displays her social consciousness by lending the car to a local charity.
Self	• Made her feel good about making a contribution to the environment.
	• Enjoyed the time she could now spend in more enjoyable pursuits.
Energy/Costs	• Gained rental income to offset the costs of owning a car.
	• She reduces the effort she needs to travel, as the car has taken over the task of driving.

Figure 19. Stephanie's Complete Story in the Value Designer Canvas

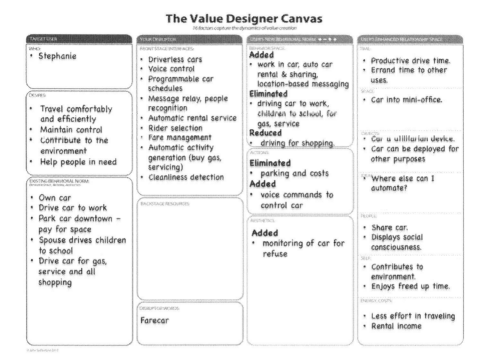

The Story Creation Process

When using the Value Designer Canvas, there are definitive patterns for the order in which it is used. First, when mapping an existing offering, it's easiest to go from left to right. However, when our task is to create an imaginary future, there is a definitive method that works best.

To create a story such as "Stephanie takes a ride," we need to learn to behave in a manner similar to playing jazz. Jazz is a fascinating music genre. As with all music, there is an underlying structure. But with jazz, the structure is minimal, a musical riff,[52] a key signature, chords and a starting rhythm. The rest is left to the players to interact with each other, feeding each other's new beats or riffs to see where the other player takes it. Imagining the future is just like that.

The disruptive scenario structure is equally simple. We have signals, which represent potential disruptors and a target user for whom we are trying to change their behavioral norm. Each disruptor has the potential to change behavior. In combination, we seek to dramatically alter someone's behavior, and in so doing, dramatically improve their relationship with their world.

Figure 20. Passing Story Elements

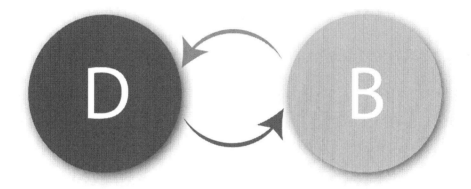

Like jazz, the two elements are like riffs that we pass back and forth. They feed off each other. The first disruptor creates some behavior changes, which in turn open the need for a new disruptor to create a complementary behavior change. Each interaction feeds the next in exactly the same way a saxophone player passes a riff to the trombone player and then gets it back. The structure never changes: disruptor to behavior, back to disruptor, back to behavior. Like jazz, the music is always different at each playing, and the story outcomes we create are never the same. That's its strength. We can imagine an infinite number of futures. If we don't like the future we created, we simply imagine a new one.

> **Key thought: Writing future scenarios is like jazz. As jazz musicians pass musical riffs back and forth, so too dreamers pass disruptors and behaviors back and forth. The first creates music, the latter, new futures.**

Some Simple Rules

Some people, when they first exercise their disruptive imagination, get bogged down and the story they imagine comes to a shuddering halt. To keep the story going, we need to keep the following rules in mind.

> **Rule 1: Everything is possible.**

This is an imaginary future. So anything goes. We should remind ourselves of this fact when we start.

> **Rule 2: Barriers are the best source of new disruptors.**

When we start to imagine barriers, which often arise, we remind ourselves again that we are creating an imaginary future. More importantly, we embrace the barrier our mind created and use it to imagine a new imaginary disruptor that can resolve the barrier. That keeps the story going. It also creates a new potential for IP if we invent the disruptor.

> **Rule 3: Build your story one incremental behavior at a time.**

Music is played one note at a time. So too, stories are built one small, everyday behavior at a time.

Disruptive Imagination in Action

Follow along as I describe the disruptive imagination I played when I wrote this story.

I started by selecting my target, Stephanie. Stephanie was a foreign bond trader I know with whom I trained for marathons. During our runs she often talked to me about getting up at 2:00 a.m to arrive before the European market opened. So I used her as the target of the story.

Next I selected a signal, driverless cars, and started asking myself questions.

"What would Stephanie do with a driverless car?" That's easy. Almost everyone would have the car drive him or her to work.

"How would her behavior change?" Clearly, she would not have to drive.

"What would she do during that time?" She would do something she can't do now: connect to the office to get a read on the European markets before they opened.

"What else would change?" She wouldn't need to park the car and pay for parking.

"What would happen to the car then?" The car could drive itself home.

"Then what would the car do?" It could drive the children to school, eliminating the need for her spouse to do that. In a later iteration,

I added that she could leave a message for the children and they could reply. That meant I had to add the message location service as a disruptor.

"Now that the children are at school, what does the car do?" The driverless car signal only took me this far. So I thought about RelayRides and came up with the idea of her automatically renting the car. At this point, I went back and added the comment about *schedule one* to the narrative to illustrate a program that allowed her to tell the car to go home, take the kids to school, and then offer itself for rental.

"What new disruptors will she need to automatically rent the car?" She will need a rental optimizer and a payment system, among others. Then my antibodies kicked in. I thought, "She wouldn't want the car to be left in a mess!"

That's a barrier. My antibodies wanted me to stop. But I didn't. I engaged with the barrier and asked myself, "What disruptors would need to be created to ensure that she only rented to people who did not leave a mess?" I thought about alcohol detection devices the police use. Perhaps they could be turned into a sniffer for bad odors in the car. That wasn't enough. Then I added video cameras to track who left behind garbage. When I added the idea that the optimizer could select from a predetermined list of clean renters, my antibodies shut off.

I iterated the story a couple more times, adding in a service disruptor that allowed for the automatic filling of gas. The car also captured the signals from today's engine diagnostics to know when an oil change was necessary. I then went to work on her relationship space changes, creating the preliminary list based on the new behavioral norm. I was checking to see how large the relationship growth would be. Large growth equals large value. After listing them, I realized the justification that she rented in order to be green could have an additional social component. So I added the idea that she sent Andrew off in the evening to help the local nursing home.

That was how the story was created. I started with one disruptor and added one behavior. Then I passed back and forth between behaviors and disruptors until I was finished. I checked the size of relationship growth to gauge how valuable the offering would be and I was done. All I needed, and therefore all we really need to create an imaginary story, are three elements:

- Signals as potential disruptors.
- The behavior changes that result from them.
- The scope of a preliminary list of relationship space changes.

These are driven by three simple rules:

- Everything is possible.
- Barriers are the best source of new disruptors.
- We build our stories one behavior at a time.

We just keep asking the same questions over and over again:

1) How would this disruptor change her behavior?
2) Where else would that behavior take her?
3) Given this behavior change, what additional disruptor would improve it?

Conclusions for Disruptive Leaders

1) Jazz works best when there are several players. So too, the disruptive imagination works best with more players. They help each other, especially when a barrier slows the story down.

2) Jazz musicians have a repertoire of musical riffs, chord changes, and rhythms, especially recent ones they've heard from other players. So too, you'll need a repertoire of signals to draw upon.

3) Learn from others. Jazz musicians copy from other musicians. So too, you should learn from other dreamers. Ask them how they came up with their stories.

4) Finally, people often remark that the imagination is a gift reserved for a few lucky souls. Bollocks! Every young child I've met has lots of imagination. If your imagination seems a little weak, it's only because you haven't exercised those muscles recently. Get started.

Exercise: Imagine a new world

1. Organize a future dream session with your team.
2. Bring a list of five or more signals.
3. Run the expert's paradox so everyone understands his or her own barriers.
4. Create a story.

Chapter 8: Now What?

No matter who, or when, or where you are, you've almost reached the end of this book. Somewhere during this read, you'll likely have reached a number of conclusions. But also, somewhere in the back of your mind, you're also wondering, "What do I do with it? How do I use this new learning? Now what?"

We are creatures of habit. We connect with all other living things through a common trait: we all consume energy. That truth holds for trees, bacteria, lions, and our species. For animals, this biological law caused the emergence of habits as a survival mechanism. Adopt a habit and you consume less energy. Consume less energy and your chance of survival increases. We can no more stop behaving habitually than we can stop breathing. Now you know why it's so hard to follow through on New Year's resolutions. Habits are hard to break. We're working against millions of years of genetic evolution.

This book described how disruptive offerings create new habits in users, the roles played to make it happen, and how entities collaborate to create the offering with significant barriers to entry behind them. It's a great recipe for sustainable growth.

However, this book also represents a potential disruptor for you. What's presented here are ideas, new ways of thinking about the world, a *be different* philosophy, if you will. Until you adopt these disruptive ideas, they have no relevance for you. They are just a few more in a series of interesting ideas that you've collected along the trajectory of your life. Only when your behavior changes, when new habits form, will this book and its ideas have meaning for you. Only then will it change your personal behavior space, and in so doing, change your relationship to your world.

That's the *now what*.

The rest of this chapter outlines new perspectives and capabilities that will start you on the journey to becoming a disruptive leader, both as individuals and in the marketplace.

THE DUAL MINDSET

The new way of thinking this book described is not intended to supplant how we think now. Rather, it is intended to add new modes of thinking.

Historically, during the early to mid 20th century, business leaders created many effective management principles, practices and methods. Those practices were created when business life cycles spanned generations. However, business life cycles are now shrinking dramatically.

Innosight conducted a study in 2012 of the S&P 500 Index that showed that the lifespans of top U.S. companies are growing dramatically shorter.

> According to their report, the 61-year tenure for the average firm in 1958 narrowed to 25 years in 1980—to 18 years in 2011. At the current churn rate, 75% of the S&P 500 will be replaced by 2027.[53]

So while business models are increasingly at risk, there still remains the need to extract as much value from existing businesses while new endeavors are cultivated. For that, we need the performance-focused practices that brought us here. But, imagining and inventing whole new businesses based on new technologies and user behaviors require different perspectives and methods. We need these new perspectives and methods because the level of uncertainty is so much higher.

Take buying a new piece of manufacturing equipment for example. The degree of uncertainty is minimal. You have a good idea of what the machine will do. You have a good idea of what it is intended to produce. You have a good idea of the volume you wish to produce. You know where you will place it in the line. While there may be variations in the numbers, the acquisition of the machine lends itself to precise calculation of ROI, pay-back period, etc.

Now compare that to the development the disruptors described in the story "Stephanie Takes a Ride." Some of the disruptors have not yet been invented. The regulatory environment is not in place. We don't know how large the market for the services might be. Nor are there any comparable offerings we can use to judge market size and acceptance. If the level of uncertainty for the machine is five, the level of uncertainty for "Stephanie Takes a Ride" is closer to one hundred.

That's why disruptive leaders have developed a different mindset to respond to the massive increase in uncertainty that making your future demands. It is also why so many leaders who are not the original founders of the business react with such strong internal antibodies. They are reacting to the massive increase in uncertainty of the disruptive idea.

So, what's needed is not to throw out existing management practices and processes that made us successful in the 20th century, but to *add* new perspectives that let us engage in disruption opportunities. This necessitates a dual mindset in the disruptive leader – a performance mindset to grow the existing business along with a disruptive mindset to capture disruptive opportunities.

Figure 21. The Dual Mindset Leader And The Blue Sky Lab

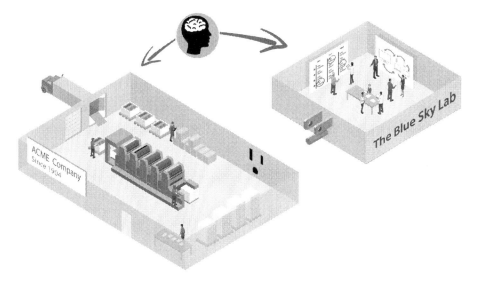

The following table highlights a sample of the new perspectives that disruptive leaders add to their existing performance mindset.

Table 5. The Dual Mindset

FROM A Performance Only Mindset	ADD A Disruptive Mindset
1. Technology makes products better for the same price.	1. Technology transforms the value equation, and creates new markets.
2. Businesses grow incrementally.	2. Businesses can grow exponentially.
3. Businesses are safe; innovate within the business model.	3. Businesses are at risk; innovate the business model.
4. Only we invent.	4. Others can invent for us.
5. We buy for greater market access.	5. We buy for emerging markets and talent.
6. We invest on ROI and NPV.	6. We invest on huge multiples.
7. Differentiate through linear performance improvements.	7. Differentiate through radically better and behavior disruption.
8. Highly planned change.	8. Learn-as-you-go change.
9. Local focus.	9. Global focus.
10. Comprehensive best in local.	10. World-class niche in local.
11. Controlling uncertainty and ambiguity.	11. Embracing uncertainty and ambiguity.
12. Certain ROI.	12. Many small bets.
13. A failure is failure.	13. We learn though failure.

Here are some tips on how to add disruptive capabilities and mindset to your organization.

TIPS ON ADDING DISRUPTIVE CAPABILITITES

It starts by evaluating where you are now.

Evaluate

Come to grips with you and your team's motivations and desires as leaders. Are you willing to learn to see the world differently, to view your business through the eyes of behavior change? How disposed are you to making yourself vulnerable by admitting that your expertise can also be your own worst enemy? Do you want to be disruptive and make a difference in the world? You need to understand what you and your team really want. Remember, your team's desire to add disruptive capabilities will determine how far down that road you travel.

Evaluate your people. Include trusted suppliers and customers on that team list. How diverse are they? How often do you hear ideas from them that fall outside the norm of your business? If not, is it because internal systems to listen shut down these ideas, or because your people only think inside the organization's frame of reference, or both?

Evaluate your people's ability to follow signs from the future and craft stories of disruptive scenarios. How well do you listen for, debate, and engage with signals of technologies that are coming but not yet available? How compelling are their stories?

Evaluate your people's ability to collaborate with other entities. How well do they embrace working with others in resolving uncertainty? How well do the reward and recognition systems provide impetus for people to engage in developing and executing bold value scenarios?

Add Listening

With an evaluation of where you are today, you can better determine how to add the following capabilities to your organization.

Purpose: install listening systems, processes and imagination. Your organization cannot become disruptive if it remains unknowing of the changes occurring outside the industry.

Listening systems

First start by creating a team of inquisitive people both inside and outside your organization. Then create a listening system. For example, Zite[54] and Evernote,[55] two free apps on tablet devices, represent a fast and easy way to get started. Zite allows a subscriber to search the web based on favorite topics. As you read Zite's feeds, you teach it what you like. Within a couple of months, it learns what feeds to send you. However, because Zite refreshes itself constantly, you lose access to your liked articles. That's where Evernote comes in. You send articles/videos you like in Zite to Evernote, which both stores and allows you to share them with your team.

Add to this "listen and store" system a list of disruptive technologies. In May of 2013, McKinsey Global published a summary of technologies expected to disrupt the global economy in the next twelve years.[56] So, when you set up your topics on Zite, use key words from the thirteen disruptive technologies McKinsey showcases to generate the feeds. Five to ten minutes a day reading and storing feeds is all the time commitment required for individuals on your team to become deeply aware of the massive disruption opportunities coming our way.[57]

Once the feeds are established, assign individual team members the responsibility to follow and document a disruptive technology. Have them use the signal analyzer to assess the relevance of the multiple signals they capture on their technology. Provide a time (so many hours per month) and small dollar amount budget for them to explore versions of the technologies that show the most promise. Walk the walk. Demonstrate in your behavior that this new activity is a must-do, not a nice-to-do.

Encourage your team members to visit universities on the leading edge of the technologies they are following. Hire students as interns from these universities to work with your team.

On a regular basis, have a team member present to the organization the disruptive technology and scenarios of how it can re-imagine a company. Use these presentations to socialize the organization that part of everyone's job is to imagine a bigger, bolder future.

Add Re-imaging

Purpose: re-imagine your business.

Encourage your disruptive team to devote a specified time regularly to create future-based value stories. Again, walk the walk. Create stories yourself, some of which are not possible today. This will force people to create ideas where invention is required.

Start this new process by boosting your team's imagining skills. Hold contests where participants are given a disruptive technology, from a listening feed, and asked to create a future value stories (like "Stephanie Takes a Ride"). The winner is the participant with the most new behaviors in the story. Repeat this exercise by pitting teams against teams.

When their skills have improved, decide on one area of the business (a customer offering, an internal process) in which a disruptive approach would produce benefits. You can start by observing users (either internal or external) and documenting the behavioral norm. Use the Value Designer Canvas to capture what you observe. Then create a number of alternative disruptive stories that will require invention. Identify a subset scenario in which an offering would fill a current need that is within reach today. Use the Value Designer Canvas to map user behavior changes. Remember, the best stories will have the most positive behavior changes. Assign the team to identify the uncertainties that will need to be resolved and your organization's contributions to them. Have them research potential partners to resolve uncertainties that your organization cannot address. Look first to trusted suppliers and customers to participate in a collaborative undertaking.

Add Engage

Purpose: inculcate disruptive thinking in selected leaders. The following activities will expose the leadership team to the new way of thinking.

Set up a lab (virtual or real) where team members are mandated to explore and commercialize disruptive opportunities. Provide a time (so many hours per month) and small dollar amount budget for them to explore versions of the technologies that show the most promise. Start small by dedicating 10 percent of your product development resources to lab work.

The key that unlocks the disruptive mindset is the ability to deal effectively with much higher levels of uncertainty than was previously the norm. The best way to learn this new mindset is to practice the "**fail fast and cheap" methodology**. Fund projects for short time frames (60-90 days) where critical uncertainties are resolved. Fail projects as early as possible. Conduct post-mortem lessons learned and reward team members for the learning that occurred.

Develop new criteria for investing in these projects. Listed below are criteria for selecting which of the scenarios developed during the re-imagine phase obtain resources to go through the fail-fast and cheap methodology.

Sample Criteria For Selecting Scenarios

1. Offering is radically different.
2. Market size can grow exponentially.
3. A small percentage (1-5%) of market provides huge returns (e.g. 20x).
4. Significant IP protection.
5. Very high margins.
6. Demographics, regulations work for you.
7. Committed board.
8. Pre-defined exit strategy.
9. A well-defined path from the first viable product into future offerings and/or target markets.

If buying into an existing company, or partnering with inventor:

1. Buy close to proof of market concept.
2. Company already raised money a number of times.
3. Your contribution is recognized in purchase price.
4. Upside to your investment provides huge returns (minimum 20x).
5. Pre-defined exit strategy.

Now What?

I started this summary by asking the question – Now what? The future is yours for the making. The opportunities to develop groundbreaking offerings and lead markets lie in front of you for the taking.

Now it is your turn!

Appendix

KEY THOUGHT SUMMARY

On Signals and Disruption

1. Signals are signs from the future about change to come.
2. All disruptions, good and bad, impact humankind in a universal way.
3. The environment in which we live shapes our behaviors.
4. Human desires are common. The behaviors we manifest to express those desires are not.
5. Disruptors create new behaviors.
6. Disruptors take many forms: objects, ideas, or processes.
7. Disruptors cause new words to be invented.
8. The environment in which we find ourselves determines our behavior universe.
9. Signals are potential disruptors.
10. The power of a disruptor is determined by how much behavior space it can create. Platform disruptors' behavior space potential grows as new devices are added.
11. Disruptors create new habits.

12. Signals and the disruptors they represent change behavior in four ways. They eliminate, enhance, reduce, and add.
13. Not all behavior space changes are equal. Eliminating, enhancing, and reducing make you *better*. Adding new behaviors makes you *different*.

On the Future and Where IP Is Created

1. We experience life in chunks.
2. The future is divided into stages of knowability.
3. Dreamers populate the imagined future with imaginary, impossible ideas.
4. The imagined future provides the impetus for innovation by creating an uncertainty framework that attracts others to experiment.
5. Inventors work in the imagined future, prototyping an impossible idea into a possible one.
6. Inventors run their experiments on supporting ideas that provide immediate returns.
7. An imagined future becomes possible when we know what we don't know and a working prototype is made.
8. Entrepreneurs organize the possible into something real.
9. Desire drives the resources required to move an idea from the imagined future to now.
10. First we dream. Then we invent. Then we organize.
11. The greatest barriers to entry are created during the imagined and possible futures. Those who participate reap the rewards of those barriers. Those who wait until it is here now are locked out.
12. The single most important strategic choice is whether to react to the future or make it.
13. Each entity has its own personal future. What's in *your* now may be in *my* knowable future.

14. Differentiation strength equals the relative value of your competitive differences times the strength of barriers to entry.
15. Adopting technologies available today offers few sustainable barriers to entry as the technology is knowable to everyone.
16. We don't lack for signals of disruptive technologies. We lack the entrepreneurs willing to take them to market.

On the Expert's Paradox

1. Like muscle memory, our personal expertise makes us extremely efficient when dealing *inside* our area of expertise.
2. In new situations, humans are sensitive to risk. Conversely, we are desensitized to opportunity.
3. In a world of increasing disruption, our biology fails us. The amygdala doesn't do engage.
4. Our expertise becomes a personal antibody when working outside our domain expertise.
5. The people best able to lead in a norm are the least able to imagine its disruption.
6. Making our personal antibodies explicitly known socializes everyone to help each other consider the possibilities inherent in disruptors.

On Value Creation

1. There are a limited number of concepts and associated questions that need be applied to successfully design a disruptive offering for any situation.
2. We receive value from an offering when it improves our seven relationships: time, space, self, people, objects, ideas, and energy.
3. We are born alone with nothing but our seven relationships. How we manage our relationships determines the quality and goodness of our lives.

4. The behavioral universe is gigantic. As creatures of habit, our personal behavior space is limited to the favored few. Offerings need to work hard to disrupt that norm.
5. All actions required to enable behavior are superfluous. Eliminating actions is *always* a winning strategy.
6. Designing an offering that pleasures the five senses is always a winner. Removing hazards (negative aesthetics) is *always* a winning strategy.

On Making Your Future

1. The future starts with good disruptive stories.
2. Writing future scenarios is like jazz. As jazz musicians pass musical riffs back and forth, so too dreamers pass disruptors and behaviors back and forth. The first create music, the latter, new futures.
3. Three rules guide the creation of compelling future scenarios.
4. Rule 1: Everything is possible.
5. Rule 2: Barriers are the best source of new disruptors.
6. Rule 3: Build your story one incremental behavior at a time.

GLOSSARY

- **Actions:** The steps taken by a user to use an offering.
- **Adoption rate:** the velocity of acquisition less the abandonment velocity.
- **Aesthetics:** The beauty, pleasures, and hazards exposed to when using a disruptor.
- **Back-stage resources:** The required assets, capabilities, and partnerships that make the front-stage interfaces functional.
- **Behavior space:** The sum of all behaviors deployed by users in the expression of their desires and goals.
- **Behavior universe:** For any given environment and time, the totality of behaviors available.
- **Behavioral norm:** The regular or habitual behaviors exhibited by an individual or group in the expression of their desires.
- **Desires:** The wants, cravings, and wishes the offering is intended to address.
- **Disruptive scenario:** A story of how someone uses a disruptive offering to improve his or her life.
- **Disruptor:** The object, idea, or invention that allows new behaviors to emerge in the expression of human desires.
- **Disruptor words:** The new terms and labels created to describe the offering or the new behavior.
- **Expert's paradox:** When disrupting, our greatest strength becomes our greatest weakness.
- **Front-stage interfaces:** The objects, ideas, processes, or combinations thereof with which the target interacts.
- **Imagined future:** The point in the future where fantastic ideas reside, where uncertainty is high but not infinite.
- **Invention barriers:** The trade secrets, patents, relationships, and other barriers to entry created in the imagined and possible futures.

- **Knowable future:** The time between now and a point in the future where uncertainty is completely known or knowable.
- **Possible future:** The point in the future when all uncertainties are known and a prototype is made.
- **Relationship space:** For any individual, the sum of all positive and negative relationships across seven dimensions: time, space, objects, ideas, people, self, and energy costs.
- **Uncertainty framework:** The questions that need to be discovered and answered to make the future arrive in the now.

BUSINESS LEADERS INTERVIEWED

George Mohacsi	President, CEO	Foresters
Shayne Smith	Vice President, International	Tetra Tech Inc.
Thomas M. Feeney	President, CEO	Safelite Group
Philip Derrow	President	OTP Industrial Solutions
Alan Homewood	Owner	2Checkout.com
Steve Byrne	Owner	Thinkwrap Commerce
Jason Cormier	Co-founder	Room 214
Heath Ritenour	CEO	Insurance of America
Stephne W. Riddell	Partner	Troutman Sanders
Joseph Caruncho	CEO	Preferred Care Partners
Karl A. Schledwitz	CEO/Chairman	Mongram Food Solutions
David Arditi	President	MIP inc.

Dwain Cox	Director of Innovation	Chick-fil-a
Eric Castro	COO	Bankers Healthcare Group Inc.
Scott Dorsey	CEO	Merritt Properties
Charles Lipman	CEO	DiversiTech Corporation
Tony Simopoulos	President	Metavera

BOOK WEBSITE CONTRIBUTORS AND COUNTRIES REPRESENTED

Contributors

David Brown, Christina Wasley, Kim Korn, Stephan M. Liozu, Eirik Johnsen, Sushil Chatterji, James Burns, John Smith, David Arditi, Thomas Kubilius, Matt Cottrill, Marie Wiese, D. R. Widder, Renata Phillippi, Linda Richardson, David Singer, Jim Dryburgh, Beto Saavedra, Berry Vetjens, Bruce E. Terry, Shana Bourcier, Kim Peiter JÃ¸rgensen, Asanka Warusevitane, Peter Troxler, Christian Labezin, Bill Welter, Bas van Oosterhout, Paola Valeri, Andrea Mason, Edwin Lee, Wolf Schumacher, Alf Rehn, Marcel Ott, Lars Norrman, Eugen Rodel, Giorgio Pauletto, Fernando Saenz-Marrero, Peter Salmon, Jenny Nicholson, Jeremy Hayes, Antonio Lucena de Faria, Goran Hagert, Frank Kumli, Chris Finlay, Shridhar Lolla, Vince Kuraitis, Linus Malmberg, Michael Lachapelle, Dan Keldsen, Abdul Razak Manaf, Martin Giorgetti, Daniel, David Hughes, Nabil Harfoush, Marc-Antoine Garrigue, Carol Wright, Vincent de Jong, Rick Bell, Alexander Osterwalder, Gareth Burton, Karl Burrow, Emilio De Giacomo, Jelle Bartels, Noel Barry, Bart Boone, Gord Hines, Richard A Mowrey, Cãesar Picos, Steve Ducat, Martin Fanghanel, Harry Heijligers, Jason King, Courtney Farina, Scott Torrance, Dave Mawhinney, Jeffrey W Letwin, Rick Horn, Jonathan Diven, Brenda Hetrick, David Vogel, Rod Vogel, Joshua Vogel, Joe Dias, Phillip Smith, Byron Hoot, Ana Balmert, Peggy Fayfich, Dr. Linda Clautti, Alisha Owens, David B. Jackley, Stephen Todd, Nikki Navta, Marc Sutherland, Marcello Figallo, Adam Shatzkamer, Sass Khazzam, Stefan Petzov, Gary Kirk, Linda Trevenen, David Elliott, Lynn Wolver, Bibianne Tessier, Alexandre Belleau, Alina Lloyd, Jari Ravelo Simmel, Erin Sutherland, Rhona Bronson, Wyman Lee, Robert Emard, Vijay Krishna, Jonathan Singer, Bob Mathias, Roger Smith, Eric Williams,

Tom Hayes, Brian Cubarney, Donald Altman, CJ Handron, Cliff Elson, Dave Banas, Barbara Da Costa, Katie Richardson, M.K. O'Neill, Jane Brazier, Darrin Grove.

Countries

Argentina, Australia, Austria, Bolivia, Canada, Chile, Finland, France, Germany, Holland, India, Ireland, Italy, Japan, Malaysia, Mexico, Netherlands, Norway, Portugal, Singapore, South Africa, Spain, Sweden, Switzerland, United Kingdom, United States.

Endnotes

[1] McKinsey Global Institute. *Disruptive Technologies: Advances that will Transform Life, Business, and the Global Economy.*. http://www.mckinsey.com/insights/business_technology/disruptive_technologies

[2] Institute http://www.jcvi.org/

[3] http://spectrum.ieee.org/nanoclast/semiconductors/nanotechnology/nanoparticle-completely-eradicates-hepatitis-c-virus

[4] The Khan Academy provides web-based learning from grade school to high schools. Based on mastery, it is already being piloted in California as a means to provide more personalized student-centric learning. Find out more here: https://www.khanacademy.org/

[5] John Sutherland, 2013.

[6] http://en.wikipedia.org/wiki/Maslow%27s_hierarchy_of_needs

[7] The first bicycle did not have pedals and was pushed by the rider's legs.

[8] Interestingly, all languages have reliable structures for the invention of new terms. They allow us to bring the unknown into the realm of the known simply by hanging some sounds on it.

[9] You can download this form at www.johnsutherlandbooks.com

[10] It may be that the disruptor used to create the behavior in the originating environment won't work in your environment. If so, how could you adapt the disruptor to work in your environment? Dr. Martin Luther King, Jr. transformed Gandhi's nonviolent resistance and applied it

during the civil rights movement. Behavior stays constant. Disruptors change to suit the environment.

[11] http://www.economist.com/blogs/schumpeter/2012/11/additive-manufacturing

[12] http://www.businessinsider.com/ge-buys-3d-printing-company-to-make-parts-for-jet-engines-2012-11

[13] http://www.economist.com/blogs/schumpeter/2012/11/additive-manufacturing

[14] http://www.economist.com/blogs/schumpeter/2012/11/additive-manufacturing

[15] http://en.wikipedia.org/wiki/Konstantin_Tsiolkovsky

[16] http://history.nasa.gov/AAchronologies/1961missile.pdf

[17] http://en.wikipedia.org/wiki/Space_Race

[18] http://www.space.com/11772-president-kennedy-historic-speech-moon-space.html

[19] Hence the purpose of this book: how to be a disruptor and not suffer disruption.

[20] The moon had millions of relevant questions. However, it was a limited number. It was not infinite. The unknowable future has infinite possibilities because there are an infinite number of possible goals with a corresponding infinite number of relevant questions to answer. Ideas in the imagined future create a limited set to resolve: the uncertainty framework.

[21] Both Robert Goddard and Werner Von Braun commented on how they had been fascinated by moon travel since early childhood because of Jules Verne's and others' books and movies on the subject.

[22] The imagined future was long for traveling to the moon, but short for the iPhone. Imagined futures can last any amount of time.

[23] Mobile phones have already arrived and NASA is working on warp drives. http://www.grc.nasa.gov/WWW/bpp/

[24] Travel to the moon remains in the future primarily because desire is lacking. Once the United States proved its technological superiority over the Soviets, Americans' desire was quenched. In the absence of

economic imperatives, there is no incentive to go back. The lack of economic incentive weighed against the cost stops other countries too. Interestingly, the companies Deep Space and Planetary Resources are exploring the feasibility of mining asteroids, now part of the imagined future. They are working to move that idea into the possible future.

[25] Technologies can be objects, processes, or ideas.

[26] You can create barriers to entry by combining technologies from today into new business models or applications. But then to do that, you have to invent something. What's important is to do so in ways that protect your IP.

[27] Back in the mid-1980s I won a President's Club trip from Xerox for the number of typewriters I sold in a quarter. Now my grandsons don't even know what the word means.

[28] http://www.fastcompany.com/1623012/will-smart-contact-lenses-be-bluetooth-headsets-future

[29] Although Microsoft is now involved, so you will have to collaborate with them. http://www.qrcodepress.com/augmented-reality-lens-from-microsoft-and-the-university-of-washington-in-the-final-stages-of-development/855942/

[30] Sloan Kettering is doing exactly that with IBM and its artificial intelligence project, the Watson Computer.

[31] http://rogers.matse.illinois.edu/index.php

[32] http://rogers.matse.illinois.edu/index.php

[33] http://rogers.matse.illinois.edu/index.php

[34] http://www.youtube.com/watch?feature=player_embedded&v=eywi0h_Y5_U - !

[35] http://www.youtube.com/watch?v=rwvmru5JmXk

[36] http://gladwell.com/

[37] Opportunities are assessed when no risk is present. In ancient times, that was a rare event.

[38] We see the same phenomenon when people move to another country and work in a different culture. The patterns in our neocortex for how to behave don't fit with the culturally accepted patterns in the

host country. That's why we feel emotionally lost. We don't know what to do and our amygdala is constantly dialing up the fight-or-flight response.

[39] Except for the young, of course, who have not yet spent the time to reach mastery. It is why they are so creative and inventive; they have so few antibodies to overcome. I am tempted to make a remark about how Western public education systems do their very best to beat the creativity out of our youth, but I will refrain.

[40] Unless, of course, your expertise lies in disruption.

[41] http://www.amazon.com/How-Create-Mind-Thought-Revealed/dp/0670025291/ref=sr_1_1?ie=UTF8&qid=1364505825&sr=8-1&keywords=how+to+create+a+mind

[42] Saying "my antibodies are screaming" works when your audience know what this means. It's a code for what kind of struggle you face. For people not familiar with the expert's paradox, you can just say that you're struggling.

[43] www.dictionary.com

[44] http://businessmodelgeneration.com/

[45] When you purchase a one dollar pencil, you are paying for the energy used to transform the California cedar tree, the graphite from South China, and the pumice powder and rubber from Southeast Asia into the pencil you buy at your local store. Likewise, your paycheck represents the collective energy you consumed in giving you the skills and knowledge you apply to doing your job.

[46] http://www.amazon.com/Blue-Ocean-Strategy-Uncontested-Competition/dp/1591396190/ref=sr_1_1?ie=UTF8&qid=1371582981&sr=8-1&keywords=blue+ocean+strategy

[47] From his book *The Innovator's Solution*

[48] That may not be as far-fetched as it seems. They have already inserted Bluetooth implants into the brains of amputees that allow them to control robotic arms. That's not so far away from instant communication.

[49] It will add a new flavor to the sense of smell and taste. Otherwise, everything else remains the same.

50 That's very normal with actions we are forced into. The action becomes habitual, and with time, normative. Because, how could there be any other way? After all, cars can't drive themselves, so we need to park them and pay for that privilege. Being forced to do something is not a behavior. It's not a "job to be done." It's an action we must take to achieve the real behavior we desire.

51 Most of the major car companies are also working on driverless cars.

52 Riff: a melodic phrase, often constantly repeated, forming an accompaniment or part of an accompaniment for a soloist.

53 http://www.innosight.com/innovation-resources/strategy-innovation/creative-destruction-whips-through-corporate-america.cfm

54 http://zite.com/ Note that at the time of this writing, Zite had been acquired by Flipboard. However, both CEOs committed to the idea that Flipboard would incorporate the topic search capabilities into the new Flipboard.

55 http://evernote.com

56 http://www.mckinsey.com/insights/business_technology/ disruptive_technologies

57 All the examples, with the exception off the space race, were found using Zite and Evernote.

Made in the USA
Charleston, SC
29 December 2016